# A Walk in the Park:
# A Vietnam Comedy

# A Walk in the Park: A Vietnam Comedy

**Odon Bacqué**

ISBN: 1515111598
ISBN 13: 9781515111597
Library of Congress Control Number: 2015911654
CreateSpace Independent Publishing Platform
North Charleston, South Carolina

To Carl Bauer
Without his encouragement and belief in me, this project never would have started. I regret that he did not live to see the completed product.

To Cookie, my wife of forty-six years
If she had not kept my letters, the memories would have remained locked inside.

To my writing instructor, Kim Graham
She awakened whatever sleeping talent exists in these pages.

To my fellow Life Writing class members
Thank you for listening to my stories and giving me both the inspiration and the advice I needed to continue.

# CONTENTS

# PROLOGUE

"**D**addy, who are you?"

I can still recall one of my girls asking me that question. I had been very fortunate in life; I had become a person of some renown in my hometown, and that was the genesis of the query.

As I started to write this story, that question came to mind, but in a different context. Now it was more existential. Who I was and who I had become was, to a great extent, the result of my being a part of the US Army and my participation in a conflict known as Vietnam. I had matured, done a job very well, and developed a feeling of self-worth. So for me, my experience in Vietnam was not a horror story; it was a great developmental experience. What I did, what I experienced, and what I learned was very important in helping me become who I am.

My stay in Vietnam was not heroic; it was much more comedic. I was, in the grunt parlance, a REMF, a "rear-echelon motherfucker."

That was not my choice; it was the grace of God, because I went over as an infantry second lieutenant. I was both Airborne and Special Forces qualified, but I went to be a platoon leader, a leader of men in battle. We were told that we would not be assigned to Special Forces because there were no second-lieutenant slots available, but we would be the best-trained platoon leaders in-country. Fortunately, as has been the case in most of my life experiences, the bad did not happen; I did end up in Special Forces but in a role I could never have imagined.

And so now, forty-four years after I returned, I have finally written the story I promised myself I'd write while I was there. The final impetus came when Cookie, my wife, and I moved into a new house three years ago, and I finally unpacked the letters I'd sent her chronicling my short army career. I wrote almost every day, and that saved correspondence helped stimulate the memories I had stored away.

But how do you start, and how do you write?

My friend Carl Bauer, who did not survive to see this finished product, encouraged me to join him in a writing class. I needed that structure and encouragement. Without both, this book would still be a future project, not a finished one.

Every veteran has his or her own story; this is mine. I was lucky, and now, through the prism of self-reflection, I can see how truly fortunate I was. And even though I was not a hero, I knew many who were and are, and I hold them in the deepest respect. My story is not meant to diminish in any way what they did but only to tell what I experienced.

For those of you who are unfamiliar with army terminology and acronyms, I have included a glossary at the end of the book.

The Central Highlands, Our Area of Operations

# BASIC AND AIT

I remember sitting in front of our black-and-white TV in the Summit Apartments, at LSU—Louisiana State University—watching CBS News report on the Tet Offensive. It was early February 1968, and I was scheduled to graduate from LSU in a few days, on the fifth of February, and then join the army on the eleventh. LSU expected me to walk down the aisle and receive my diploma, but I had made a deal with the army recruiter. He had written the university a letter telling them that I would be in the army on graduation day and unavailable to personally receive my diploma. I was actually going to be in Red River, New Mexico, skiing—my last "fling" before becoming a soldier. My mom, who had been subject of many pranks, did not believe I had actually graduated until the diploma came in the mail several months later.

You would think that I would have been worried, since my army career was only a few days away from starting, but I was completely unconcerned. Why? I had been told that because of my eyes (I was almost blind without glasses) I could not be in a "combat arms" position. I was, the recruiter stated, probably bound for an embassy in an exotic locale. I would first have to go through basic training, an advanced course, and finally infantry-officer courses, but that was just a formality, leading to an assignment in the Adjutant General's Corps. Based on those reassurances, I had not one twinge of concern as I watched the bullets hitting in camera range.

I had arrived at this position because of a law-school request that I not return for my second year. I had finished my first semester on probation, and the second semester sealed my fate. Because I had transferred to LSU from USL, The University of South Louisiana, as an undergraduate, I lost a semester and had gone to law school without a degree. In the summer of 1967, I received a letter from Uncle Sam letting me know that if law school didn't want me, he did. Since I lacked only a semester to graduate, I was able to delay the draft until my graduation, scheduled for February 1968. With that small issue decided, I started to investigate my options. Both my grandfather and father had served as military officers, and I thought that might be a good way for me to serve as well. I knew there was a war going on, but I just did not think that I would be part of it. There was no justification for my belief; it was just the way I reacted to the situation.

The first options I investigated were the reserves, but because of the end of the 2S school deferments, the smarter people had closed that option to me. One reserve unit had openings, but it was a Special Forces unit, and you had to be a paratrooper to join. I had, since a very young age, a great fear of heights, and just the thought of jumping out of a plane terrified me.

I looked at the navy and air force, but in the back of my mind, I felt that the army was my destiny. Because of my desire to be an officer, I had to appear before a panel of army officers to be interviewed. After they asked me many questions and looked at my medical records and the thickness of my glasses, they said that, in their collective opinions, I would be unfit for a combat assignment, which was certainly music to my ears. Once again my charm, wit, and intelligence, as well as my physical limitations, had rewarded me, or so it seemed. I signed the papers and waited for school to end.

On the eleventh of February, a beautiful early spring day, I was sworn in to the army in New Orleans. My parents and fiancée, Cookie, were by my side. I was dressed in a sport coat, tie, and penny loafers. After the swearing in, I was told to catch a plane at the airport, leaving at 6:00 p.m., and given an envelope full of paper.

My destination: Fort Dix, New Jersey.

The four of us spent a very pleasant afternoon in New Orleans, and I was delivered to the airport in good spirits. I later found out that this freedom was most unusual, but at the time I thought nothing of it. In most situations, the draftees were delivered to the airport or bus station in locked buses and under guard. I guess the army figured that a volunteer, dressed in a sport coat, was not a flight risk. When I left New Orleans, the temperature was in the low sixties, and I felt a sense of adventure as I boarded the plane.

I arrived in Philadelphia at about midnight; the temperature was in the twenties, snow covered the ground, and an unheated blue school bus was waiting for me. It was about half full, but because of the darkness, it was difficult to make out what my companions looked like. When we got to Fort Dix at around 2:00 a.m., we were shown in to a brightly lit classroom filled with hippies and other nefarious-looking characters. I remember looking around and knowing for certain that I was in the wrong place. I went up to a sergeant and told him that there had been a mistake. I was going to Officer Candidate School (OCS) and was sure I did not belong with the others in the room. He looked at me for a second, and then he announced in a loud voice that there was an "officer candidate" in the room and that he—meaning me—was uncomfortable with his surroundings. I immediately realized I had made my first tactical error and quickly learned a very important lesson. I never mentioned OCS again.

After a sleepless night filling out paperwork, our first trip was to the barbershop, where my already short hair was completely removed. The barber was nice enough to ask my preference before he shaved me, but it made no difference—everyone got the same cut. The next few days were a flurry of activity: getting our gear, shots, and physicals and shipping home our civilian gear. When our fatigues, boots, and jackets were given to us, we were asked our sizes. At that time my waist was about thirty inches, and I wore a medium shirt. I was given forty-inch pants and an extralarge shirt. I had to wait three weeks to get an outfit that actually fit.

After three days of KP, an assignment that was given to me because I had mentioned OCS in the reception station, I was assigned to a basic training unit.

We were stationed in brick barracks with only six men to a room. We had a bed and side table, but all of our possessions were kept at the foot of the bed in a footlocker. We were taught to make our beds, wear our uniforms properly, and shine our boots and brass. From sunup to late night, we were forced to run, fight, crawl, march, and shoot. Any of these that we did not know how to do, we were taught. Our instructors used threats, fists, and screams to completely intimidate us, and then they praised us when we finally got it right. It was February in New Jersey, so it was cold, and everyone was sick. But we weren't allowed to spend any time in sick bay unless we were in imminent danger of dying. We were also subject to daily inspections of our footlockers, weapons, and uniforms. It was impossible to live up to the expectations of the drill instructors, but that was part of the training psychology. Marching was another feat that almost did us in. It was hard to imagine that a person could confuse left and right, attention and parade rest, and right-shoulder and left-shoulder arms, but all of us did. And then one day, almost magically, we got it right.

Basic training was designed to destroy our individuality and build us back up as part of a unit. This was accomplished by making us do mindless tasks that made no sense, but we did them anyway. In our basic-training company, there were many who were planning to attend OCS. There were also quite a few who were planning to desert at the first chance. One person actually did leave, but he was soon caught and returned to camp. To my knowledge, no one liked basic, but we managed to persevere. Our nemesis was always the drill instructors, who found glee in making our existence as hellish as possible. One instructor, Sgt. K, supposedly went through lockers, stealing from the troops. It never happened to me, but I heard it from too many people for it not to be true. We actually ran into him again in OCS, when we were senior candidates. He was in the basic class there, and we were able to give some payback.

Some of us began to excel in different areas. I ended up shooting an "expert" score on the rifle range. I was not surprised, as I had been hunting since I was a child, but a lot of the cadre was sure that someone wearing glasses as thick as mine had no chance of hitting even one target.

After eight weeks of torture, we graduated. I was twenty pounds lighter and years wiser.

Our next assignment was advanced individual training (AIT); for me that meant infantry, and I was fortunate enough to qualify as a truck driver. That meant that for most training exercises, I was driving instead of marching. The only negative was that I had to wake up an hour early to get the vehicle from the motor pool and stay up an hour later to return and wash the vehicle when we were finished. But even missing that extra sleep was worth the ride.

One day, when I was in the company area, I heard a Cajun accent yelling out, "Where you at, mon?" The question was not directed at me, but it made me immediately curious about who was here, in New Jersey, from back home. As I asked the group of guys where they were from, they realized that I was from Louisiana as well. "We from Breaux Bridge, mon, and we all in de national guard, doing our training. Where you from?" After finding out I was from Lafayette, about fifteen miles from Breaux Bridge, the next question was as expected: "Who's your daddy?" After discussing our family lineage and finding out we were not related and had no common acquaintances, we bade each other good day.

I never saw them again.

Our barracks area was in a very different part of the post, and our accommodations were also quite different. Now we were in some old World War II barracks, with forty men to the barracks. There was no insulation in the walls, and there was little heat. We were a lot tougher since finishing basic, and the rate of colds and sniffles went down dramatically. I had a top bunk, which was much harder to make up. The daily inspections continued, but most of the time, we were passing.

Here our infantry skills—patrolling, marksmanship, map reading, and tactics—were practiced until they became second nature. In the army, if the chain of command is broken during battle, every soldier is encouraged to take charge if he has no immediate superior to depend on. This, in my mind, is one reason our units were such good fighters; we allowed anyone to lead if he had to and gave him the skills to do it. I found myself becoming very comfortable in this environment. I began to, if not enjoy, at least tolerate the training.

Finally, in late May, we graduated from AIT, and about ten of us had orders for Fort Benning, Georgia, where we were destined to attend OCS. We had a few weeks before our OCS class started, so I went home for my first visit in four months. I was at home when Martin Luther King was shot, and I saw the rioting on TV. There was talk that our OCS class might be delayed and we might be deployed in the worst trouble spots, but fortunately that did not happen. Several of my fellow classmates, who were also going to OCS, planned to pass through Lafayette on their way to Fort Benning, and I asked my parents to host a pig roast for us in our backyard. I lined up dates for all the guys, and we ate and drank until late in the evening and then turned in, knowing that the next day we were leaving for Columbus, Georgia, and the next chapter of our army training. I was still unconcerned about my ultimate assignment because the army had made a promise to me. How could they renege on that?

# OCS, PART 1

The summer of 1968 was brutal in the South, and there was no place hotter than Fort Benning, Georgia, where I was to attend OCS. In spite of that fact, I remember my feelings of excitement as I drove through the gate to the post, thinking that twenty-five years prior, my dad had done the same thing. I couldn't help but wonder how he felt as he entered the base for the first time. I was also thinking that this could be an adventure, somewhat like grown-up Boy Scouts. But I was mistaken.

My first stop was to the tiny officer quarters of Lt. Woodrow (Woody) Dixon, my LSU roommate. Woody had gotten married a few weeks before, and Cookie and I attended his wedding. He was now at Benning for the officer basic course. He seemed somewhat embarrassed when I saluted, but he was a lieutenant, and I was then an E-5 sergeant. We visited awhile, and then I bade him good-bye and went to report. I was assigned to Fifty-Fourth OCS Company, which meant I was in the fifth battalion and the fourth company in that battalion. At that time there were three OCS battalions, each consisting of four companies. Each company had about 150–175 cadets to start, significantly fewer at graduation. All of the barracks were in a central area of the post, directly across the street from the Airborne track and towers. We were assigned to our rooms and told that classes would start the next day early.

In the middle of the night, a group of senior cadets from a neighboring company rousted us out of bed and subjected us to several hours of harassment. Most of it was purely physical, push-ups and dying cockroaches, but some of the seniors were sadistic and cut up our boots and uniforms. I have always thought that this type of behavior has no place in leadership training.

The next morning we were up for PT and overall orientation. At mid-morning we were gathered into an assembly area, between our barracks and our neighbors, and were addressed by Capt. Yoshita, our company commander. It was obvious from his Japanese accent that he was not a native, but he was wearing a silver star, so he was "for real." He began his speech by introducing himself and then making what I thought was obviously an incorrect statement.

He said, "This is infantry OCS, and all of you will be infantry officers. There will be no branch transfers."

Since my recruiter had promised me the Adjutant General's Corps, I knew that what he was saying could not be true, but I did feel a hint of apprehension.

I was assigned to the First Platoon, as each platoon member was assigned alphabetically. The barracks were in excellent shape, made of freshly painted cinder block, and all were two stories. First and Second Platoons were on the bottom floor, and Third and Fourth were upstairs. There was both a front and rear entrance, but we never used the front. A courtyard was situated outside the back entrance, between our building and a twin building adjacent to us. The senior candidates who made the harassing run were located in the twin building. In the middle of the building, running lengthways, a main hall separated the building in half. The bedrooms faced that hall, with two or three candidates assigned to each room. My roommate was Roy Budd, who went on to helicopter flight training after OCS. His goal was to survive Vietnam, and then set up a helicopter business in New York City; I have never checked to see if he was successful.

OCS was a twenty-six week course, and though the academics were rigorous, mental stress was the primary hardship. Being able to maintain your equilibrium, under the most difficult circumstances, was essential.

If you were successful in finishing the course, you were obligated to serve two years from the date of graduation. Many of our classmates decided that was too much time to spend in the army and believed an early visit to Vietnam was a better alternative than the additional time in the service.

Our OCS class was one of the first since the abolition of the 2S deferments, which made our class almost 100 percent college graduates, with several master's degrees and one PhD thrown in as well. That much education made training difficult for our instructors, as we all asked questions regarding why we had to do things "this way."

Several of us had been in AIT together, so we were not all strangers. This was both advantageous and challenging. Part of OCS involved peer reviews, where we had to grade the best and worst in our platoon. Since it was much easier to give poor grades to those we didn't know, the first few evaluations were not based on merit. This caused a problem later on for Bob Bruce, who became a good friend but was not part of our AIT group.

The days developed into a routine of reveille at 5:00 a.m., PT at 5:30 a.m., breakfast at 7:00 a.m., and classes starting at 8:00 a.m. We were back in the barracks at 6:00 p.m., had dinner at 6:30 p.m., and then studied until lights-out at 10:00 p.m. We were expected to keep our uniforms starched and pressed all day—no matter what physical exercises we were engaged in—our boots spit shined, and our barracks immaculate. The main hall was to be spit shined as well, so we decided that we would only walk on the tiles closest to the wall and only in stocking feet, so we wouldn't have much to polish each day. The floors in our rooms were also expected to shine, so we became adept at moving from door to bed to desk without walking on the floor. Our foot-lockers and lockers were supposed to be ready for inspection at any time, and each morning our uniforms, brass, and boots were closely inspected. Since most of us were in our twenties and pretty smart, it became a game to see how many rules we could break and not get caught.

Our adversaries were the TAC officers, who were newly graduated second lieutenants. Each platoon was assigned one, and ours was Lt. Bowman, a former Green Beret sergeant who had decided to go to OCS. He was a great officer and knew all of the tricks. Many times we'd be plotting our next prank only to turn around and find him standing there. How he moved so quietly was always a mystery, but it added to his mystique.

We remained "basic candidates" for the first twelve weeks, and then we were promoted to intermediate status. That continued for the next six weeks, and then we "turned blue" and became senior. There were increasing privileges along the way, and as senior candidates we were almost officers—we thought we had it made, but that was not always the case. All during the twenty-six-week period, we had candidates dropping out. By the time we graduated, the class size had dropped to close to one hundred graduates, with over a 30 percent dropout rate. Those who dropped out had an immediate transfer to Vietnam. I had made my mind up that I would never quit, although there were times when I thought I was stupid to stay.

Most of our days were spent either in a classroom or in the field, learning how to lead men in battle. Even though I was not going to be an infantry officer, I enjoyed the classes and the training and found myself doing well. Unfortunately, this would affect my ultimate assignment.

Just after becoming intermediate, in the twelfth week, each of us was required to fill out a "dream sheet" where we indicated in which branch of the army we desired to be placed. It was called the "dream sheet" because it supposedly had no relationship to your actual assignment. Because we were so impressed with Lt. Bowman, two of my good friends, Bill Brooks and Dick Bowley, put Airborne and Special Forces as their choices and showed them to me. They seemed to be challenging my courage, so I also put down Airborne and Special Forces and added Adjutant General's Corps, in that order, which came back to haunt me. I knew I could not be in a combat arm because the recruiter told me that my eyes were too bad, so what was the harm in putting down Airborne and Special Forces? In the meantime I continued to do well in both class and field problems, and I was enjoying the camaraderie.

While I was busy learning how to be a soldier, Cookie was equally busy teaching school and planning our wedding while living with her parents in Lake Charles, Louisiana. We got engaged a few months before I graduated from LSU, and Cookie had planned our wedding for December 14, four days after I was supposed to graduate from OCS. She chose not to check with anyone of authority to make sure I would be available, just knowing in her soul that the army would never stand in the way of intended nuptials. Everything was blissful, so far.

Because of the high temperatures, many days were spent in a "heat alert" that limited physical activity. No one complained, though, as marching was much better than running. Because of the need to "break starch" every day, the laundry was a very popular location. We had to pay for the services because there was no time or facility to do laundry on our own. Several of the cadets were married, and their wives could deliver a week's worth of laundry on the weekend, but the single guys had to tend to that task themselves.

For the first twelve weeks, we had no passes and very little free time. What free time we did have was mostly spent in line at the laundry and PX. We were forbidden to eat civilian food, so sneaking a candy bar, beer, or hamburger became as important as learning to wage a conventional war. This is where Lt. Bowman's skills at snooping and pooping became our bane. For the married cadets, who desperately wanted conjugal visits, even more legerdemain was needed. Since we were confined to post, they needed to find secluded places on the base where they could "visit" with their wives. Several were caught at the target ranges by the MPs, but no one was expelled for it, just made to march punishment tours.

Our time was mostly spent in the routine of PT, class, study, and sleep, day after day.

In the twelfth week, we were allowed to have a dance to celebrate the turn from basic to intermediate. That occurred in the early fall, and Cookie drove from Lake Charles, accompanied by another candidate's wife, who was living at Fort Polk, about an hour away from Cookie.

It was great to see her and hear her stories about her teaching job and the wedding preparations. All the candidates seemed to enjoy themselves, as this was our first chance to really relax. Bob Bruce and I wrote and starred in a farcical piece about an OCS candidate's life, and it was well received by all; even the TAC officers were observed to smile. The weekend ended too quickly, and the routine returned.

I found myself doing very well in weapons, tactics, and land navigation and not so well in adjusting artillery fire and PT. I was also doing well in "leadership," which was a very subjective talent, somewhat like beauty is in the eye of the beholder.

Lt. Bowman rotated out on his way to Vietnam, as did most of the other TAC officers. Other than Lt. Bowman, the officer I remember best was Lt. Melancon, from Beaumont, Texas. He left to go to Airborne school, and we often saw him marching with the other trainees to run on the Airborne track or go to the three-hundred-foot towers. Those towers were directly across from our barracks, and we could easily see the trainees being pulled to the top and then released to float to the earth. The floating, however, was sometimes interrupted by a crosswind, which could blow the parachute into the tower, collapsing the canopy. If that happened, the rate of fall would increase dramatically and could lead to death. The army realized this fact and installed hooks on the legs of the tower to "grab" the canopy and keep the recruit suspended, potentially saving his life. When this occurred, someone had to climb the tower, rescue the trainee, and remove the canopy. Watching this occur made me very secure in my belief that anyone who chose to jump from a plane was stupid, at best, and I was very thankful that I was unfit for regular combat, much less the role of an Airborne soldier.

# OCS, PART 2

As we labored, learning to become officers, the days seemed to creep by. Our numbers were diminishing weekly as cadets either chose to quit or were asked to leave. I continued to do well and was reasonably secure in the knowledge that I would never see Vietnam. As we approached the eighteenth week and senior-candidate status, the excitement built within our company. Senior status meant we were probably going to graduate and our daily lives would become easier.

Turning senior, or blue—so-called because we were allowed to wear a blue ascot, a blue circle on our helmets, and blue shoulder patches—was a big deal. We were saluted by junior candidates and presumed to be a rank just below second lieutenant. Our days consisted of more class and less field time. Fall was in the air, and Fort Benning was becoming bearable. To celebrate our senior status, we had a formal dinner dance. This was also part of our training, as we had to learn how to go through a receiving line and the proper etiquette to use in genteel company, something that we did very little of in regular training. Cookie again came to visit, and she was beautiful in her long dress. Almost all the cadets had dates or wives in attendance, and once again Bob Bruce and I put on a skit, pillorying the OCS experience. Again it was well received, even though the tactical officers were the butt of our jokes.

Shortly thereafter I heard that Bob Bruce was being dismissed from the class for "lack of leadership." Bob was short and somewhat stout and had no military bearing. Even after wearing freshly starched fatigues, he looked rumpled. He was, however, very bright, and in my opinion, he had acquitted himself well. Bob was devastated by the news. I pulled him aside after our evening meal, and I told him I would try to get the decision reversed.

"How in the hell are you going to do that?" he asked me.

"I'll use my selling skills to sell you."

"Bacqué, if you pull this off, I will forever be in your debt."

"Just invite me to visit you in New York when this is all over and we are civilians again."

"I'll throw you and Cookie the biggest party ever thrown in Fishkill, New York."

I went to our company commanding officer to speak on Bob's behalf and laid out my arguments, including giving examples of other cadets who, in my mind, had not performed as well as Bob. Bob was the victim of a peer-review system that forced us to rank all of our peers, and Bob had a low ranking. The CO told me that my arguments were valid, but the decision was made at the battalion level; I would have to visit with the battalion commander, a lieutenant colonel.

I was nervous as I knocked on his door and was told to enter. I had prepared my arguments, the same ones I had used on the CO, but here I was speaking to someone I had never met before and who had a great deal of rank on me.

I saluted and stood at attention.

"At ease, candidate; what is this about?"

"Sir, I feel a great injustice is being done to Candidate Bruce. He has performed well in every area except leadership, according to the CO, and he is recommending, based on that issue, that Candidate Bruce be dropped from OCS. The CO has placed Candidate Bruce in numerous leadership positions, trying to prove him unworthy, and in my opinion, Candidate Bruce has performed well. There are several other candidates who, in my opinion, have done a lesser job than Bruce but who have a more regal military bearing, and they are not being singled out."

"So you think that the problem with Candidate Bruce is that he doesn't look like an officer?"

"Yes, sir, I do. I do not think that looking like an officer should be a criterion."

The colonel, a portly man himself, looked at Bob's file, which he had on the desk in front of him. It seemed like I stood and waited forever, but in reality it was only a few minutes. He looked up and said, "I think you are right, Candidate; I see nothing in this file that would be grounds for dismissal. The most I will allow is a two-week delay in graduation, but I don't think that will happen."

Bob was ecstatic when he graduated with us. He was killed in his first week in Vietnam. I wonder—if I had not argued for him, would he still be alive today?

The last test of OCS was the "Ranger Problem." In this exercise, our company would split up into four platoons and wander through the Georgia woods and fields for two weeks. This was scheduled for early November and would end just before Thanksgiving. We left our barracks on a Sunday afternoon, a beautiful Indian summer day. Because of the weather and the fact that sleeping bags weighed about ten pounds, many of my classmates decided not to carry theirs. For some reason I don't recall, I brought mine along. As we entered the woods, the leaves were still changing, and the view was beautiful. I was in charge of navigating our platoon to our first bivouac and getting us there before dark. I had always excelled in land navigation, but this was a lot harder. Still, we made it to our location with time to spare. Our TAC officer told me he was impressed with my performance. As we bedded down, we could see lightning and hear thunder. Unbeknownst to us, an arctic front was on the way, and the weather would become our greatest enemy. That night it stormed, and we huddled under our shelter half, trying to keep dry. We were on a 25 percent watch, which meant that three-quarters of the platoon could sleep while the other quarter pulled two-hour watches. As the night dragged on, the temperature started falling, and by morning, it was in the thirties. Luckily for those who'd left their sleeping bags at the company area, during the two hours that those of us who had the bags were pulling watch, they were able to use ours, but they had to keep moving from bag to bag. Those of us who had carried the extra weight were very happy we did. During the rest of the exercise, the temperature never rose above freezing, and we were not allowed to build fires, as they might reveal our location to the "enemy."

The object of the problem was to mimic battle conditions as closely as possible without inflicting true casualties. To that end, many members of our group were captured or "killed" by the "enemy" Ranger forces as we moved endlessly through the Georgia woods. Bill Brooks, Dick Bowley, and I managed to escape and evade all attempts to eliminate us. As the two weeks were starting to end and our misery was starting to really weigh on us, we reached a swampy area. Our orders were to cross the swamp, though the temperature was still hovering around the freezing mark. When we questioned the sanity of breaking ice to cross a swamp on foot, we were told that to quit would endanger our graduation. I am sure it was colder during the battle of Bastogne, but I cannot imagine being more miserable than we were crossing that swamp. We had already lost several classmates to frostbite, and this was even worse. We all made it through the swamp, but we were not allowed to warm up.

That afternoon, we were visited by the commanding general of Fort Benning, whose name I do not recall. I do know that he called the remaining survivors into a formation and did the same for the Rangers. He then began to lambaste the Rangers, as well as our OCS training cadre, for being idiots at causing the amount of injuries our company endured. One of the first caveats of command is to criticize in private and commend in public. This was the first ass-chewing I had observed during my short time in the army, and it was epic. That night we bedded down in tents and were allowed to build several large bonfires. Even then the Rangers harassed us by driving jeeps through the compound and firing M-60 machine guns, filled with blanks, several times during the night. The next morning trucks picked us up and took us back to the barracks; the Ranger Problem was finished. Bowley, Brooks, and I had done well and were complimented.

By the end of the Thanksgiving holiday, all of the hospitalized troops had returned, just in time for the next big event—the reading of the orders, which would tell us what our next assignment would be and also give me an idea of whether I would be able to attend my wedding. We had two weeks to go until graduation.

# ENGAGEMENT PARTY

Our wedding, as I mentioned before, was scheduled for December 14, 1968, four days after graduation. My grandmother, who considered herself to be part of "Old Lafayette Society," decided to have a party to introduce Cookie, who was from Lake Charles, to her fellow society members. This party would be held on the Saturday following Thanksgiving, a short two weeks before the planned wedding and my graduation. Since I would be a very senior cadet, I thought surely I would be allowed to come home for both Thanksgiving and the party. The planning by my grandmother and aunt was done with no regard for army rules or regulations; they'd just based it on blind faith. And even if I couldn't make it, Cookie would be there. She was the one who needed to be introduced; I was already known.

As I have previously stated, because of weather conditions and poor execution, the commanding general had reamed out our OCS cadre in front of our company and had created ill will between them and us. I suspect this is why we were confined to base for the Thanksgiving holidays. I was forced to tell Cookie that there was no way I could go home to be with her at the party. This caused her much grief, as she knew no one in Lafayette and did not want to attend without me.

On the Sunday preceding Thanksgiving, we were allowed to make phone calls from a phone booth in the entry hall of the barracks. The line was always long, so we tried to limit the length of our conversations. When my turn came and Cookie and I started to talk, I could sense an excitement in her voice.

"Donnie, I have great news. I think you will be able to attend the party."

"Cookie, that is impossible, I told you that we are confined to post. I am not going to be there."

"I think that Sam and Jake have got things worked out," she said.

Sam was her dad, and Jake Haxthausen was his favorite drinking buddy. Sam and Jake met every evening after work for a beer and gossip at Prejean's Bar, a typical Cajun beer hall. In fact, I was introduced to Sam, by Cookie, at Prejean's.

At that instant, a cadet rapped on the door to the phone booth and announced that the company commander wanted to see me "right away."

I said, "Cookie, I have to report to the company commander."

Her reply of, "Great!" left me puzzled.

I knocked on the CO's door and was summoned in.

"Candidate Bacque reporting as ordered, sir," I said, standing at attention and saluting.

Usually the reply would be "At ease, Candidate," allowing you to assume a more relaxed position; that statement never came. He returned my salute and said, "Bacque, what have you done?" in a very stern voice.

"Sir, Candidate Bacque, I don't understand the question," I replied.

"I understand you got a girl pregnant and need to go home, this weekend, to marry her," he answered.

Then I started to understand Cookie's reply and the trouble she could be getting me into, just so I could attend the party.

"Sir, Candidate Bacque, you are mistaken. I am getting married in a few weeks, and I can assure you that she is not pregnant and I am not required to go home to marry her this weekend. There is a party that my fiancée would like me to attend, and I told her that my attending was impossible. The two issues must be related."

"Well, Candidate Bacque, it seems we have a problem because a congressman has contacted the post commander and asked that you be allowed to attend your wedding, so you need to explain to the battalion commander, so he can send the reply up-channel. He is expecting you now. Dismissed."

I saluted again and left the office wondering how much trouble I was in.

As I walked to battalion headquarters, I tried to imagine what had happened. I knew that Sam and Jake were involved, but how could it have escalated to this level, and how had a congressman gotten involved? And most importantly, how would this affect my pending graduation?

I reported in to the duty officer, who announced my presence to the lieutenant colonel battalion commander, the same one I had spoken to on behalf of Bob Bruce. I do not recall his name, but I do recall the conversation.

I entered and saluted, remaining at attention again.

"I don't recall seeing any candidate twice during OCS, and I am getting tired of seeing you, but tell me this, Candidate Barkew [his tortured pronunciation of my name], who do you know?"

"What do you mean, sir?"

"Well, we're not used to getting calls from congressmen, and I just want to know who you know."

"Honestly, sir, I am as much in the dark as you. What I do know is that there is no one pregnant, and I do not have to attend my wedding this weekend."

"Well, Candidate Barkew, I can't tell you not to go home because a congressman has personally requested that we allow you to go, but I would consider it a personal favor, since there is no wedding, that you remain on base with your classmates."

"Sir, I am happy to oblige, since I never planned to go home anyway."

"Thank you, Candidate, and you are dismissed."

Once again I saluted and left.

As I walked back to the barracks, I was still confused and anxious to speak to Cookie and get the real story. When I got there, the phone booth happened to be empty, and I immediately called Cookie.

"Are you coming?" she asked.

"No, and you almost got me in a lot of trouble. Please tell me what happened."

"Well, Sam and Jake were at Prejean's, and they knew how upset I was that you wouldn't be at the party, so they started brainstorming to see if there was a solution. Jake said that he knew Congressman Edwin Edwards well enough to ask for a favor, and Sam said to make the call. That is all that I know."

Later I found out, after speaking to Sam and Jake, that Edwin knew the regimental CO, a Col. Piper, rumored to be a member of the Piper Aircraft family. Edwin was a pilot and owned a Piper airplane. I assumed he had met Col. Piper because of that connection. I can only imagine how that conversation had gone:

"Colonel Piper, Edwin here."

"Congressman, how are you doing?"

"Fine, but I need a favor."

"Anything—what can I do?"

"You've got a Louisiana boy in OCS who needs to go home for a wedding party, and he can't get leave. His bride-to-be is very upset, and I need this boy to go home."

"Give me his name, and consider it done."

As in the parlor game that we played as children, by the time the message got down several layers, it was garbled beyond comprehension.

I did not attend the function, but Cookie did, wearing black as her way of protesting. None of the attendees seemed to care; they just had a great party, except for her.

And since I did graduate, it did not affect my army career.

# OCS, PART 3

Friday, November 29, 1968, was auspicious for several reasons. First, it was the Friday following Thanksgiving; second, it was the day before my twenty-fourth birthday. but most importantly, it was the day that we, the cadets of the Fifty-Fourth Company, would receive our orders. There was palpable excitement as we gathered on that overcast morning in formation to hear our assignments. For many of us, these orders would determine whether we lived or died. I was amazingly nonchalant, as I recall, since my only concern was what embassy would be my next duty station. We would be graduating on the tenth of December, a little over a week away, and we knew that all the rough stuff was over and now we waited for "the rest of the story."

The formation was called behind the barracks, and we were lined up by platoons, standing abreast. The captain stood on the back steps, looked us over, and then began the call. As was the case in almost every army situation, the orders were called out alphabetically.

"Airborne," shouted the captain. There was a slight pause, and then the names were read out:

"Alderson," pause, "Bacque," and then all sound was blocked out.

When I heard my name, my heart seemed to burst, and it was as if someone had kicked me in the stomach. How in the hell could I be assigned to Airborne when I was not suited for combat? Besides that, there was the fact that I was deathly afraid of heights; how could I jump out of a plane? I felt like I was going to be ill. Some terrible mistake had been made, but how? Then I remembered the dream-sheet request I had turned in during the twelfth week. They told us that it made no difference what we requested, but it must have made some difference. Could I tell them that I was just kidding around with Brooks and Bowley? My mind was racing, but no answers were coming.

Before I could stop hyperventilating, the captain shouted, "Special Forces," pause, "Bacque." I was first on that list, along with Bowley and Brooks. Special Forces, the Green Berets—that was even worse news. I wasn't exactly sure what Green Berets did, but I was aware that it involved a fair amount of danger, as did jumping out of airplanes. The only bright spot in the whole ceremony was that I was to report for Airborne training, my next duty assignment, on January 5, which meant that I would be available for the wedding Cookie had planned for December 14—if she didn't kill me before that date.

As the formation broke up, after being dismissed, Brooks and Bowley came to congratulate me. I suspect they could see the shock in my face and asked how I felt. I told them honestly that this was a terrible mistake and asked for help in trying to get the orders changed. They looked at me like I was crazy.

"Let me see, Bacque," Brooks said. "You want to tell the army that you were just kidding around when you did your 'dream sheet' and that you want to change their minds about your future assignment. Is that correct?"

"You bet."

"And who will you go to, to make this request?"

"The CO, I guess."

"And where will he send you and your request?"

"The battalion commander?"

"How happy will he be to see you?"

"I'm getting the point. I guess I'm just as screwed as you are."

"That's right, Bacque, and we will love it! By the way, when are you going to tell Cookie?"

"Oh, shit, she knows we were going to find out today and wants me to call as soon as I know; I just can't tell her on the phone. I need to figure something out."

"You're the salesman; let's see you sell Cookie."

I showed Brooks one of my fingers as I turned and walked away.

That evening, I made the call to Cookie.

After dispensing with the pleasantries, Cookie asked, "Did you get your orders? What embassy will we be going to?"

"Cookie, you won't believe this, but they misplaced my orders and are looking for them. But I am sure that I can be home for the wedding."

"Well, I'm happy about that, but I would feel better if I knew where we would be going next."

"As soon as I know, I will let you know."

I had decided that, despite my enormous selling skills, there was no way I could sell Cookie, on the phone, that this assignment was good news. Besides, I needed to find out what exactly a Green Beret did and what that might mean for me.

Brooks and Bowley were in the same predicament but felt much better about it. Both were single, and I guess they did not mind the specter of death. I, on the other hand, was getting married and very much wanted to survive my army experience. Besides, the army had reneged on its unwritten promise, made to me by the recruiter. I had to figure this all out.

Since a big part of army life involves alcohol and we needed to be well trained in all aspects of army existence, we were allowed to frequent the officers club located in our training area.

One evening, shortly after our orders were given to us, we ran into a new lieutenant who was wearing a Special Forces patch, at the bar. He had been in Special Forces as a sergeant and was authorized to wear the patch on his sleeve to show prior service.

As we related to him our pending assignments, he said that we shouldn't worry because we would never be in Special Forces in Vietnam. It was a very small unit, and there were no second lieutenants in the table of organization. Then he looked at me. He said, "You look Spanish—do you speak Spanish?"

"My mom is from Puerto Rico, and I can get along in Spanish, but I am certainly not fluent."

"Well, they might keep you because they have some operations going on in Bolivia, and they are sending every Spanish-looking person there."

"What are they doing in Bolivia?" I asked.

"That is classified; but if you are chosen, you will find out."

I wasn't chosen, but I did find out that the operation was to eliminate Che Guevara and his communist threat. I certainly would have seen more action there, had I been chosen. But now I had my sales pitch for Cookie: South America. She had majored in Spanish, and I knew that the prospect of South America would thrill her. But it had to be a face-to-face conversation, so until I got home, as far as she was concerned, I had no orders.

I did tell Dad and swore him to secrecy. He was planning to come for my graduation, and we would drive back home together.

Dad arrived on the ninth, planning to spend the night, attend graduation the next day, and leave with me as soon as the ceremonies were complete. Because of graduation preparations, I could not meet him at the airport. I picked him up at the hotel the next morning. He was reading a book titled *The Devil's Brigade*. It was a story of a predecessor special operations organization in which the casualty rate approached 100 percent. He showed me the book and said, "You really got yourself in deep shit this time; you're probably going to die."

That wasn't quite the encouragement I was looking for, and I told him not to worry. "I've got it figured out."

He would have to wait until after I told Cookie what I thought might actually happen. I had planned to tell him first, but his attitude pissed me off.

We went to graduation, and I graduated on the Commandant's List, in the top 10 percent of the class. I found out that if you were on the list, you were given your first choice of assignments. Well, no one asked me what I wanted, and then I remembered the "dream sheet." Had I listed Adjutant General's Corps first, Cookie and I probably would be headed to an embassy instead of Airborne school. Lady Luck had deserted me on that issue.

Dad and I left Georgia around noon and arrived home about 9:00 p.m. Cookie was at my home in Lafayette, waiting for me—and the news of our pending assignment. After a passionate kiss, she asked, "Where are we going?"

"Cookie, you won't believe this, but it looks like we're going to South America."

I could see the light in her eyes as she repeated, "South America?"

"It appears that it will be my final assignment, but first I have to go to Airborne school at Fort Benning for three weeks."

"But after that, South America?"

"Well, before we go to South America, I have to go to Special Forces school at Fort Bragg in North Carolina."

I could see Dad frowning and knew he was wondering how I was going to pull this off.

"But after that school, South America?"

"Cookie, that is what they are telling me—that because of my Spanish heritage, they need people like me in South America, but with the army, as you know, nothing is guaranteed."

"But you feel good about what they told you?"

"I don't think they would lie to me again."

"No, I guess not. That is wonderful news."

At least I had a six-month reprieve until the next set of orders came, and who knew, it could have been South America.

Let the wedding festivities begin.

# THE WEDDING

Cookie had picked Saturday, December 14, 1968, as our wedding day, which meant that it was preceded by Friday the thirteenth. I am not a superstitious person, but an awful lot of bad stuff happened that day.

I spent Wednesday at home, buying a car and making my arrangements, while Cookie went back to Lake Charles to make the final preparations for the wedding. Lake Charles is located about seventy-five miles west of Lafayette and is a pretty city located on a beautiful lake. If the description ended here, it would be one of the more desirable communities in the country, but unfortunately there is more to the story. Lake Charles is a port city, and the main products are related to agriculture and energy. The agricultural commodities do not detract from the charm, but the energy sector does. Lake Charles, and the lake that borders it, is surrounded by several large petrochemical plants that paint the sky with dark ash, emit a putrid odor, and light the night sky with large candles of burning gas. But it was Cookie's home, and we were getting married there, no matter what.

On Thursday, John Sorli, one of the groomsmen, arrived from Air Force OCS, where he was in the middle of trying to become an officer, a task that would turn out to be too steep a hill. John was a native of New York State, was a graduate of the University of Connecticut, and had been my roommate during my aborted effort to finish law school. John flunked out the first semester, but he was having so much fun that he never informed his mom of that outcome and ended up staying the spring semester as well. With no classes to attend and plenty of distractions, John became a big one for me. I suspect I would have been asked to leave anyway, but John helped seal my fate. And when we were dismissed from school, our draft status went from 2S to 1A. Both of us received draft notices within the next few months.

John was a night owl, doing his best work from midnight on. He then slept from dawn to dusk. The military is not forgiving of those whose schedules do not fit its own; thus, John's attempt to become an officer was hopeless.

On Friday we all went to Lake Charles, where my family had reserved a block of rooms for the weekend. Cookie had planned a "small" wedding: only seven bridesmaids and a guest list that approached five hundred. I was allowed to invite fewer than twenty of my friends, as Dad had his own ideas about who "needed" to be invited.

That afternoon we were fitted with our tails and all the trappings that went with them. That was when bad luck began to intrude.

"Donnie, I can't find my black shoes," John Sorli announced.

"John, why didn't you mention this earlier when we could have bought or rented you a pair?"

"I didn't realize the problem until I started to look for them."

"John, every pair of shoes you wear in the service is black; you don't have one pair somewhere?"

"Well, I might have a pair in my car trunk, but they are really in bad shape."

I opened his trunk—a huge space littered with detritus from years of hoarding and storing, and found a raggedy pair of black shoes. They did look bad.

"John, you are going to have to polish these shoes."

"I have never been very good at polishing anything; you don't want me to polish them. Can't we get them polished?"

"OK, John, first thing tomorrow morning I will find a barbershop and get them polished. The wedding isn't until two o'clock." The first crisis seemed to have been averted.

That night we had the rehearsal dinner for the out-of-town guests and wedding party as well as the relatives my parents had invited, most of whom I had never seen before. The fact that it was boring—and long—allowed the wedding party to become well lubricated before the dinner ended. Then we wanted more activity, so someone said, "Let's go to Quinn's." Quinn's was a seedy joint, located near the port of Lake Charles, which was frequented by merchant seamen. Quinn was known for his racist jukebox and dancing in his Ku Klux Klan robes. Going there was not an intelligent decision, but all intelligence had long left the group. As our loud and obnoxious crowd entered the bar, a silence descended. The occupants were not happy with the obviously intoxicated guys who were in our group, but the girls looked interesting. If we had been thinking straight, we would have left then, saving us a lot of grief, but we stayed. The girls were asked to dance, and the guys were ignored.

Cookie, who had the least amount to drink of everyone, decided she wanted to go home and made me leave with her. The rest of the group stayed; I planned to return after dropping Cookie at her home. Later, while I was gone, an altercation had broken out. No one could recall for sure how the fight started, but all survived, though somewhat the worse for wear.

As I brought Cookie to the door, it was still Friday the thirteenth. She abruptly opened the door, walked through, and slammed it in my face. I was a little taken aback, but since I had had a lot more to drink than Cookie, I decided not to make a big deal of it.

I headed back to Quinn's, not knowing that we were no longer welcome, and saw my brothers heading my way quickly. I flashed my lights, and they stopped. That's when I found out about the fight and also learned everyone was OK.

It was now the morning of the fourteenth, albeit very early in the morning, and we decided to find another bar. The name and location of that place is lost in memory, and my next recollection is awakening in our hotel room and spotting a trash can next to my brother's bed, with his head suspended just above the rim. It appeared that he had need of a receptacle during the night and had left it there as he slid back into sleep. The stench in the room rivaled that of the petrochemical plants, and the prospect of a beautiful wedding day seemed wishful at best. I still had the Sorli black-shoe problem, so I awakened him and had him accompany me as we searched for a bootblack. In the meantime, one of the bridesmaids was hosting a brunch for the bridal party, and we

had a strict timetable for my arrival, as I was not supposed to see Cookie until the actual ceremony.

We got the shoes shined, went back to the hotel, got my brothers up and showered, emptied and washed out the trash can, and made it to the brunch on time. Fortunately, or unfortunately, there was alcohol there as well, and we all drank up. Then we headed back to the hotel, where we dressed for the ceremony, and drank more on the way to the church, Our Lady Queen of Heaven. I can truthfully say that I had never before, or have ever since, consumed the amount of alcohol that I did over that twenty-four-hour period, and it came back to haunt me.

The ceremony was, I am told, beautiful and relatively brief. The reception was at the Lake Charles Country Club, a lovely facility located on a promontory jutting into the lake, with a stunning view. Several sheriff deputies, who probably had been looking for us the night before, escorted us to the reception. One of them, I found out, was an old boyfriend of Cookie's.

The band was great, the food delicious, and the bar well stocked. A very good friend of mine, George Wimberly, was in the wedding, and his father was as talented a clarinet player as Pete Fountain. George came up to me during the reception and said, "My dad has his clarinet and would be happy to play a few songs for you."

Several hours later he was still playing, but Cookie and I had a flight to catch. We attempted to leave the party, but my dad had neglected to turn off the headlights when he drove my car to the reception. The battery was dead, so we had no ride. Then Deputy Wayne Bono, Cookie's old boyfriend, said, "Don't worry. I'll bring you in my vehicle, and we can get home fast because I have a siren."

As we proceeded toward town, at a high rate of speed, Wayne handed us a champagne bottle from a case he had left the party with. Drinking helped to calm our nerves, and soon we were at Cookie's. As Cookie and I dressed in our going-away outfits and Wayne finished the bottle of champagne, I heard a siren wail. It seems that Kay Hartiens, the wife of Andy, who was one of the ushers and a very close friend, had discovered that Wayne left the cruiser unlocked and the keys in the ignition, so she went for a ride around the block. According to her, that was the most exciting thing she had done so far in her life.

When Cookie and I finished dressing, we had to leave for the airport and our flight to New Orleans, where we would spend our first night as husband and wife. Once again Wayne fired up the cruiser, siren, and lights and, drinking from another bottle, led a parade of cars to the airport. When we arrived and parked, we all proceeded to the terminal building. As luck would have it, Gov. John McKeithen had just arrived in Lake Charles for a function and was exiting the terminal as we were walking in. My brother Frank, who had been continuously overserved since Thursday, ran up to the governor and said, "Governor, I can't believe you came to see Donnie off; come over here, and say hi to Donnie and Cookie."

The governor, probably thinking that this was an assassination attempt, scooted away with his bodyguards. The Lake Charles paper, however, covered his arrival, and the paper's photographer, who noticed the melee, was able to snap a photo of Wayne Bono drinking from the bottle of champagne while in uniform. Wayne was retired from the force the next day.

In 1968 there were no security lines or security protocols, so as Cookie and I boarded the plane for New Orleans, the entire wedding party did so as well. Finally the stewardess announced that anyone not planning to go to New Orleans had to disembark, as the schedule was very tight. With that announcement, the party exited, and the cabin door was closed. The two gentlemen sitting in the seat just in front of us turned and asked, "Did you just get married?"

As I attempted to say yes, I vomited all over my new going-away suit and caused most of the passengers some extreme discomfort for the rest of the flight. What a way to start married life! Was this a harbinger of things to come? I was certainly hoping not.

As it turned out, we have been married for forty-five years, so no harm done.

Now for the honeymoon!

# AIRBORNE SCHOOL

Early the next morning, Cookie and I left for Puerto Rico, my mother's childhood home. Airborne school was not scheduled to start until January 4, so we had almost a month off after the wedding. A lot of my relatives still lived there, including my grandparents, so there was much family socializing going on, in addition to the honeymooning. After returning from Puerto Rico, we prepared to move to Fort Benning, Georgia, my first duty station. I would be there for three to four weeks, trying to become a paratrooper, unless I died of fright before.

We drove to Fort Benning in our new Pontiac that I had purchased just before the wedding. Although it was a four-door sedan, I had installed the latest in electronic wizardry, an eight-track tape player, in a vain attempt to make it "cool."

We left in the early morning, just at daybreak, Cookie and I, accompanied by Sir Patrick, our new dog. Sir, his common name, had never been on a highway trip before, but what could go wrong in the backseat? The trip to Benning took a day, with numerous stops for both Cookie and Sir to use the facilities. I did notice some bumping on the back of my seat during the trip but thought Sir was just bored and amusing himself. It wasn't until we arrived at the base and unpacked the backseat that I noticed the dog had eaten all the ribbing off the back of the seats—not a pretty sight. Cookie, who was already doubtful of the wisdom of bringing a dog into our newly wedded life, was pretty upset, but we were still in love, and she soon forgot that incident.

We moved into a small apartment just outside the base gates and set up housekeeping, all three of us. The apartment was about the size of a large closet, and since I would be gone from dawn to dusk, Cookie and Sir had to adapt to life together. I reported to the Airborne school at 5:00 a.m., which meant getting up about 3:30 a.m. Cookie insisted on rising as well and fixing me breakfast, an effort I did appreciate. She would drive me to the school, drop me off, and then go back to spend her day with Sir. She would come back to the school to pick me up at 6:00 p.m.; I would be bone-tired. We would have dinner at 7:00 p.m., go to bed by 9:00 p.m., and then repeat the routine the next day. Ask her how she liked our first few months of marriage.

I, on the other hand, was learning how to do parachute-landing falls (PLFs), how to properly exit from an aircraft, and most terrifying of all, how to be released from the three-hundred-foot tower, the same tower I had observed with trepidation during OCS. This training occurred during our first two weeks, with the third week reserved for actual parachute jumps. I found that the PLF and exit training were relatively simple, but when we drove to the towers, I was petrified.

The cadre lined us up—I was somewhere in the middle of the line—and started the process of sending us up the tower. This involved being strapped into a parachute harness, which was attached to a real parachute canopy. The canopy was attached to a frame that held it open, in a deployed manner. The canopy frame was attached to a cable that would lift the frame to the top of the three-hundred-foot tower. When you reached the top, the canopy would stop, for about a minute, and you would hang there. Then, the cable would be pulled up rapidly, for about three feet, and that would cause the canopy to release and allow the student to drift slowly to the ground. It sounds innocuous, but in reality it was the most frightening part, for me, of the entire school.

"Bacque, you're next."

My heart was in my throat, and I could barely breathe.

"Step up here, and we'll strap you in. Is it too tight?"

How could it be? I figured the tighter, the more secure.

"Could you make it tighter?" I replied.

"That's as tight as it can go."

"OK."

"Are you ready?"

My mouth was so dry I could not speak, so I just nodded my head.

"Here you go!"

Several of the guys who went before me commented on how great the view was during the trip up. I would have to take their word for it because my eyes were shut tight.

When the canopy reached the top and paused for a minute, I did open my eyes, and the view was great, but the minute the canopy started up, I closed them again. After a hard jerk, I could feel myself drifting down, not a stomach-churning feeling, like a roller coaster, but just a gentle drop. That prompted me to open my eyes and start guiding the chute away from the tower. For sure I did not want to find myself hanging from the tower as I had observed many other trainees during OCS.

When I finally touched the ground, did my perfect PLF, and immediately regained my feet, the cadre sergeant congratulated me on my performance and told me that if we had enough time, I could go again. As soon as he turned his back, I hid behind an ambulance that had been placed there in case an accidental hard landing occurred. There was no way I was going to try that another time.

Finally "Jump Week" arrived. The number of Airborne students had diminished by about half, but our entire OCS group had made it—Henry Alderson, Bill Brooks, Dick Bowley, Kevin Marinachio, and Dennis Manarchy. Now it was time to put all our training to use or die trying.

Since this was the third week in January and conditions had to be right to allow us to jump, there were numerous delays due to inclement weather. Many days had us suited up, ready to board the plane, only to have the flight canceled because of low overcast and high wind conditions. Finally, when the weather cooperated and the first jump was imminent, I was so bored with the scrubbed jumps that I actually forgot my fear.

We loaded onto the aircraft in two rows, sitting across from one another and facing each other. The plane lifted off and turned toward the drop zone, at most a fifteen-minute flight. About five minutes out, the jumpmaster started his instructions:

"Get ready. Stand up."

We did.

"Hook up."

This meant hooking your static line to a cable running the length of the plane. Failure to do this would cause a very fast fall—and an unfortunate ending.

We did hook up.

"Check equipment."

This meant checking your own equipment to make sure everything was tight and ready, as well as checking the person in front of you, as he could not check his back.

We did.

"Sound off for equipment check."

We counted off, "One OK," "Two OK," "Three OK," and so on, until the entire side had sounded off.

Then the jumpmaster told the first man, "Stand in the door."

That person had to be ready to jump as soon as the red light beside the door turned to green. If he hesitated, it meant that the last people exiting the aircraft might miss the drop zone and land in the trees. To stand there, for what seemed like hours but in reality was only thirty to forty-five seconds, was hellish. I only had to do it once, and that was plenty for me.

Finally the light changed, and the jumpmaster yelled, "Go!" as each of us exited. If you were in the middle of the "stick" (the line), all you saw was the man in front of you moving, and you were right behind. As he reached the door, handed his static line to the jumpmaster, turned into the door, and exited—encouraged by a swat to the behind by the jumpmaster—you were next.

As I exited the aircraft in a tight position, I could feel the wind buffeting me. I remember counting four seconds: *one thousand one, one thousand two*. At one thousand four, you were to look up and check your canopy. I did, and it was beautiful, completely open and regulating my rate of descent. As I looked around, the sky was full of parachutes, the plane noise was rapidly diminishing, and I was floating above the earth. The feeling was blissful and serene, not at all the terror I thought I would experience.

n, several Thai officers, who were fluent in French, approached
pted to engage me in conversation. Not wanting to be rude, I
erstanding very little, smiled when they did, nodded when asked
estion, and as soon as possible excused myself. I still wonder to
they asked me and what they think I replied.

-ons continued and were great consumers of time, as well as
y. But finally we started the officers' course. In Special Forces,
ere supposed to understand the capabilities of the men in their
d have a rudimentary skill in each of their individual expertise.
sisted of twelve men—two officers and ten enlisted—with two
ssing the same proficiency in weapons, communications, intel-
cine, and engineering/demolitions. The teams were formed in
at they could be split into two and still have all the individual
six-man team.

icers' course, we received an overview of the team members' ca-
we were tested in how well we were able to utilize them in mock
uations.

cushy job doing walk-ons, getting back into a training condition
e reported early, did PT, went for a five-mile run through the
hen attended classes the rest of the day. Running was never my
run through the woods was timed. If you took more than fifty
were out of the program. Again, it was a struggle, but I never
myself to think about quitting.

eantime, Cookie had gotten hired as a substitute teacher, and
ney she was earning really helped. We were both still harboring
vould end up in South America, but as I talked to people who
ow, the fighting there was as bad as Vietnam. Che Guevara was
of that operation, and he was well guarded by a group of local
es. Cookie, I could tell, was not convinced we were going due
d started to worry.

eantime, I was happy with the coursework and the new friends
. The one who stands out the most in my memory is Richard
was rumored to be the shortest man in the army. He was a first

But then I saw the ground rapidly approaching, and it was time to land. I did not do a perfect PLF, but it was passable, and I was still alive. How great was that?

We needed to do five jumps before we were ready to graduate, and all, for me, were relatively uneventful. On the second jump, one of the jumpers did have a malfunction, and the cadre on the ground, seeing this occurring, screamed up through a bullhorn to pop his reserve. So five jumpers—four of whom had no problems—popped their reserves.

But the fifth jump offered the most comical relief.

For that one we were placed in a C-141, a jet aircraft. Because this was unlike any of our other jumps and there were some potential problem areas, we were briefed prior to takeoff.

"Gentleman, this jump will be different. Because we are jumping from a jet, you are not supposed to make a vigorous exit. If you do so, your chute could be sucked into the jet exhaust and melt. You do not want that to happen. Also, we will be moving much faster than a prop plane, so there is a special wind door to protect you as you jump. This may sound dangerous, but don't be concerned."

Easy enough for him—he wouldn't be jumping.

As we entered the aircraft, I was positioned next to Henry Alderson, an OCS classmate. After we sat down, I turned to him.

"Are you concerned?"

"Not in the least," he replied, "a piece of cake."

As we stood, ready to exit the aircraft, Henry turned to me and smiled and then walked to the jumpmaster, handed him his static line, bowed his head, and turned to exit, not noticing he was one step too far back. As he walked to where he thought the door was, he walked into the side of the plane, bounced back, shuffled to his right, and made his exit. Watching him completely distracted me from the fear I felt, and I made my last required jump with no mistakes.

Then we were through and were presented our jump wings at a nice graduation ceremony. Cookie got to pin them on. Now I was a paratrooper, the first step toward becoming a Green Beret, and heading to South America.

Next stop: Fort Bragg.

# FORT BRAGG

Now that we were officially paratroopers, it was time to report for specialized training. Henry Alderson, Kevin Marinachio, and Dennis Manarchy were heading for the Eighty-Second Airborne, while Brooks, Bowley, and I were going to Special Forces, but all of us were heading to Fort Bragg. That being the case, we did a convoy. Our destination was Henry Alderson's house, where Cookie and I could stay until we found our own place to live. Henry had a small ranch-type home with a fenced backyard. Cookie and I were given one of the kids' bedrooms to sleep in, and Sir was put in the fenced yard. Sir, finding the stress of the trip, the strangeness of the surroundings, and the barking of Henry's dog unnerving, barked the entire night. There was nothing I could do or say to get him to settle down. I knew we needed to find a house immediately.

One common factor of every military establishment is the transient nature of the inhabitants. That means that usually rental properties are easy to find. That does not mean, however, that suitable rentals are available. But, once again, luck was with us, and we found a pretty, little ranch-style home for $300 per month. Since my base pay was $500 per month, with an extra $110 per month Airborne pay, the $300 was a stretch. We did have free medical and could shop in the commissary. I am not sure how we did it, but we lived pretty well on my income, in spite of the extravagant rent.

Brooks, Bowley, and I were assigned to the training detachment, but our training course would not start for six weeks, so we were temporarily assigned to Third Special Forces Group. We could wear berets, but we had no group "flash" on them, just a ribbon indicating the training detachment. For the next

six weeks, there was very little to do, so our da[...] though we were volunteered to test parachutin[...] cept at that time. We also were included on s[...] we sat around, studying the history and geog[...] assigned mission.

One day our detachment commander, a c[...] speak a second language. I told him that I had [...] in school and, though not fluent, could speak[...] He gave me a script, written in French, and [...] did and was immediately "hired" to become [...] Special Forces demonstration called an "A-Te[...] Gabriel Group. In this demonstration, the det[...] would lead his team onstage, and each membe[...] specialty and mission in both English and sec[...] Spanish natives in Special Forces but no Fren[...] was chosen. I became Capitaine Bacque, le C[...] I was a captain, even though my rank was s[...] real beret as well as captain's bars and was sen[...] and festivals to show off "my detachment." M[...] walking around the special warfare center ur[...] sure they were wondering what I was doing. b[...] involved in special warfare (snooping and po[...] me to ask what in the heck I was doing dress[...]

My fondest memory was appearing at th[...] Spivey's Corner, North Carolina, which was [...] our team made it on national TV—quite h[...] masquerader.

Since most people did not actually speal[...] cellent, I was never questioned—until the d[...] came to the Special Warfare School. That da[...] a stage in the auditorium with both visiting [...] manding officers looking on. Capitaine Bac[...] ful impersonation of a French-speaking ca[...]

demons[...]
me and [...]
listened[...]
an obvi[...]
this day [...]
The [...]
very eas[...]
the offic[...]
commar[...]
The tea[...]
enlisted [...]
ligence, [...]
that way[...]
talent in [...]
In th[...]
pabilities [...]
battlefiel[...]
After [...]
was toug[...]
woods, a[...]
forte, and [...]
minutes, [...]
once allo[...]
In th[...]
the extra[...]
hope tha[...]
seemed t[...]
the objec[...]
revolutio[...]
south and [...]
In th[...]
I was ma[...]
Flaherty, [...]

lieutenant, back from a tour in Vietnam with the 101st Airborne Brigade. He wanted to become a Green Beret, but a great impediment was his inability to swim. I remember watching him jump into the pool and sinking directly to the bottom, where the training cadre finally pulled him to the surface. They took him away for a while, but a few days later, he rejoined us and did graduate with the class.

On one of our later field exercises, where we parachuted in, Flaherty hurt his back and was trying to find medication to help the pain. We had a doctor going through the course with us whose last name was Duda. I remember him as being a vet, but Brooks thinks he was a cardiologist. Anyway, he was on the operation with us and gave Flaherty some aspirin to help with the pain. As an aside, forty years later Flaherty looked me up and asked me if I remembered the jump, as well as his injury. It appeared that he was applying to the VA for benefits and needed a witness. I was happy to help.

Since I was the only one married in our close circle of friends and Cookie, even back then, was a wonderful cook, our house became the gathering point for my loose-knit circle of friends. Cookie never knew whom I would drag home, but she was always a sport about it.

Finally we were ready to graduate, but the last big test was a two-week problem in the piney woods, called Robin Sage. We were supposed to parachute into an unfriendly country, link up with some insurgents, help them destroy communications and infrastructure, and avoid being captured by the enemy forces. Because I had grown up with a lot of exposure to the outdoors and was very proficient in both map reading and using the compass, I really enjoyed these kinds of exercises, especially since this occurred in the late spring, when the weather was beautiful. My group was never in danger of being discovered or captured, and we had an excellent evaluation upon the termination of the problem.

Now we became real Green Berets and were issued our Third Group flash. Bowley and I were assigned to a field unit, while Bill Brooks went into the admin section. We all knew that sooner or later orders would be issued, but we were told that we would never be assigned to Special Forces in Vietnam because there was no slot for a second lieutenant in Special Forces, so all of us would be going somewhere else. This would all happen before we became first lieutenant, which would occur on December 10. In those days rank was automatic—you were a second lieutenant for a year and then a first lieutenant for a year. If you stayed in, you became a captain when you finished your second year as an officer. So we would not be in Special Forces in Vietnam when we went, but we would still be much better trained than our infantry-school classmates, and chances were that we might not die as quickly. (All that seemed fine to me because I was still going to South America.)

As a field unit, we were expected to train in the field. That meant jumping from planes carrying full gear, setting up camp, and "snooping and pooping." On one operation we had a captain who did not seem too sharp. He sent three of us, all lieutenants, on a recon mission. We found a highway, flagged down a car, and caught a ride to a corner grocery. There we bought a case of beer and carried it back to camp, where we hid it in a stream. We invited our friends to take a walk with us and sample some of our treasure. By evening I was barely able to talk and was wondering if the captain would suspect anything. Luckily he was not sharp, and nothing ever was said, so I guess in this singular incident, we got away with it.

I also brought a fishing rod and reel along. It was one that was collapsible, and I could fit it in my rucksack. I caught a bass that evening, before I was too drunk to fish, and I cleaned and roasted it over the fire. I had fresh fish while the rest of the group ate C rations.

As the summer wore on, rumors began circulating regarding orders for all of us. We knew that we had to get them soon or we might not have enough time left in our enlistment to serve a year in Vietnam. Finally, in July, they were issued. Bowley and I were on a set with fourteen other second-lieutenant classmates for Vietnam. Brooks was going to Jungle School, his choice, and then joining us in-country.

I went home that evening dreading sharing the news with Cookie. Over a glass of wine, I broke the news and was surprised at how calmly she received it. She explained that she had a sixth-sense belief that we would not be going to South America, so she was not shocked by the orders. I was to report to Oakland, California, for deployment on September 15, 1969, but I was given

But then I saw the ground rapidly approaching, and it was time to land. I did not do a perfect PLF, but it was passable, and I was still alive. How great was that?

We needed to do five jumps before we were ready to graduate, and all, for me, were relatively uneventful. On the second jump, one of the jumpers did have a malfunction, and the cadre on the ground, seeing this occurring, screamed up through a bullhorn to pop his reserve. So five jumpers—four of whom had no problems—popped their reserves.

But the fifth jump offered the most comical relief.

For that one we were placed in a C-141, a jet aircraft. Because this was unlike any of our other jumps and there were some potential problem areas, we were briefed prior to takeoff.

"Gentleman, this jump will be different. Because we are jumping from a jet, you are not supposed to make a vigorous exit. If you do so, your chute could be sucked into the jet exhaust and melt. You do not want that to happen. Also, we will be moving much faster than a prop plane, so there is a special wind door to protect you as you jump. This may sound dangerous, but don't be concerned."

Easy enough for him—he wouldn't be jumping.

As we entered the aircraft, I was positioned next to Henry Alderson, an OCS classmate. After we sat down, I turned to him.

"Are you concerned?"

"Not in the least," he replied, "a piece of cake."

As we stood, ready to exit the aircraft, Henry turned to me and smiled and then walked to the jumpmaster, handed him his static line, bowed his head, and turned to exit, not noticing he was one step too far back. As he walked to where he thought the door was, he walked into the side of the plane, bounced back, shuffled to his right, and made his exit. Watching him completely distracted me from the fear I felt, and I made my last required jump with no mistakes.

Then we were through and were presented our jump wings at a nice graduation ceremony. Cookie got to pin them on. Now I was a paratrooper, the first step toward becoming a Green Beret, and heading to South America.

Next stop: Fort Bragg.

# FORT BRAGG

**N**ow that we were officially paratroopers, it was time to report for specialized training. Henry Alderson, Kevin Marinachio, and Dennis Manarchy
were heading for the Eighty-Second Airborne, while Brooks, Bowley, and I
were going to Special Forces, but all of us were heading to Fort Bragg. That
being the case, we did a convoy. Our destination was Henry Alderson's house,
where Cookie and I could stay until we found our own place to live. Henry
had a small ranch-type home with a fenced backyard. Cookie and I were given
one of the kids' bedrooms to sleep in, and Sir was put in the fenced yard. Sir,
finding the stress of the trip, the strangeness of the surroundings, and the
barking of Henry's dog unnerving, barked the entire night. There was nothing
I could do or say to get him to settle down. I knew we needed to find a house
immediately.

One common factor of every military establishment is the transient nature
of the inhabitants. That means that usually rental properties are easy to find.
That does not mean, however, that suitable rentals are available. But, once
again, luck was with us, and we found a pretty, little ranch-style home for
$300 per month. Since my base pay was $500 per month, with an extra $110
per month Airborne pay, the $300 was a stretch. We did have free medical and
could shop in the commissary. I am not sure how we did it, but we lived pretty
well on my income, in spite of the extravagant rent.

Brooks, Bowley, and I were assigned to the training detachment, but our
training course would not start for six weeks, so we were temporarily assigned
to Third Special Forces Group. We could wear berets, but we had no group
"flash" on them, just a ribbon indicating the training detachment. For the next

six weeks, there was very little to do, so our days were spent mostly at leisure, though we were volunteered to test parachuting out of helicopters, a new concept at that time. We also were included on some training hikes, but mostly we sat around, studying the history and geography of Africa, Third Group's assigned mission.

One day our detachment commander, a captain, asked if any of us could speak a second language. I told him that I had taken both French and Spanish in school and, though not fluent, could speak both languages rudimentarily. He gave me a script, written in French, and asked me to read it to him. I did and was immediately "hired" to become a detachment commander for a Special Forces demonstration called an "A-Team Walk On," better known as Gabriel Group. In this demonstration, the detachment commander, a captain, would lead his team onstage, and each member of the team would describe his specialty and mission in both English and second language. There were many Spanish natives in Special Forces but no Frenchmen; that, I suspect, is why I was chosen. I became Capitaine Bacque, le Chef du détachement. In this role I was a captain, even though my rank was still second lieutenant. I wore a real beret as well as captain's bars and was sent all over North Carolina to fairs and festivals to show off "my detachment." Many of my friends would see me walking around the special warfare center uniformed as a captain, and I am sure they were wondering what I was doing. but because Special Forces was so involved in special warfare (snooping and pooping), no one ever approached me to ask what in the heck I was doing dressed like that.

My fondest memory was appearing at the National Hollering Contest in Spivey's Corner, North Carolina, which was covered by Charles Kuralt, and our team made it on national TV—quite heady for a twenty-four-year-old masquerader.

Since most people did not actually speak French and my accent was excellent, I was never questioned—until the day some officers from Thailand came to the Special Warfare School. That day we did our demonstration on a stage in the auditorium with both visiting dignitaries as well as our commanding officers looking on. Capitaine Bacque—that's me—did a wonderful impersonation of a French-speaking captain, and after we finished the demonstration, several Thai officers, who were fluent in French, approached me and attempted to engage me in conversation. Not wanting to be rude, I listened, understanding very little, smiled when they did, nodded when asked an obvious question, and as soon as possible excused myself. I still wonder to this day what they asked me and what they think I replied.

The walk-ons continued and were great consumers of time, as well as very easy duty. But finally we started the officers' course. In Special Forces, the officers were supposed to understand the capabilities of the men in their command and have a rudimentary skill in each of their individual expertise. The team consisted of twelve men—two officers and ten enlisted—with two enlisted possessing the same proficiency in weapons, communications, intelligence, medicine, and engineering/demolitions. The teams were formed in that way so that they could be split into two and still have all the individual talent in each six-man team.

In the officers' course, we received an overview of the team members' capabilities, and we were tested in how well we were able to utilize them in mock battlefield situations.

After the cushy job doing walk-ons, getting back into a training condition was tough. We reported early, did PT, went for a five-mile run through the woods, and then attended classes the rest of the day. Running was never my forte, and the run through the woods was timed. If you took more than fifty minutes, you were out of the program. Again, it was a struggle, but I never once allowed myself to think about quitting.

In the meantime, Cookie had gotten hired as a substitute teacher, and the extra money she was earning really helped. We were both still harboring hope that I would end up in South America, but as I talked to people who seemed to know, the fighting there was as bad as Vietnam. Che Guevara was the objective of that operation, and he was well guarded by a group of local revolutionaries. Cookie, I could tell, was not convinced we were going due south and had started to worry.

In the meantime, I was happy with the coursework and the new friends I was making. The one who stands out the most in my memory is Richard Flaherty, who was rumored to be the shortest man in the army. He was a first lieutenant, back from a tour in Vietnam with the 101st Airborne Brigade. He wanted to become a Green Beret, but a great impediment was his inability to swim. I remember watching him jump into the pool and sinking directly to the bottom, where the training cadre finally pulled him to the surface. They took him away for a while, but a few days later, he rejoined us and did graduate with the class.

On one of our later field exercises, where we parachuted in, Flaherty hurt his back and was trying to find medication to help the pain. We had a doctor going through the course with us whose last name was Duda. I remember him as being a vet, but Brooks thinks he was a cardiologist. Anyway, he was on the operation with us and gave Flaherty some aspirin to help with the pain. As an aside, forty years later Flaherty looked me up and asked me if I remembered the jump, as well as his injury. It appeared that he was applying to the VA for benefits and needed a witness. I was happy to help.

Since I was the only one married in our close circle of friends and Cookie, even back then, was a wonderful cook, our house became the gathering point for my loose-knit circle of friends. Cookie never knew whom I would drag home, but she was always a sport about it.

Finally we were ready to graduate, but the last big test was a two-week problem in the piney woods, called Robin Sage. We were supposed to parachute into an unfriendly country, link up with some insurgents, help them destroy communications and infrastructure, and avoid being captured by the enemy forces. Because I had grown up with a lot of exposure to the outdoors and was very proficient in both map reading and using the compass, I really enjoyed these kinds of exercises, especially since this occurred in the late spring, when the weather was beautiful. My group was never in danger of being discovered or captured, and we had an excellent evaluation upon the termination of the problem.

Now we became real Green Berets and were issued our Third Group flash. Bowley and I were assigned to a field unit, while Bill Brooks went into the admin section. We all knew that sooner or later orders would be issued, but we were told that we would never be assigned to Special Forces in Vietnam because there was no slot for a second lieutenant in Special Forces, so all of us would be going somewhere else. This would all happen before we became first lieutenant, which would occur on December 10. In those days rank was automatic—you were a second lieutenant for a year and then a first lieutenant for a year. If you stayed in, you became a captain when you finished your second year as an officer. So we would not be in Special Forces in Vietnam when we went, but we would still be much better trained than our infantry-school classmates, and chances were that we might not die as quickly. (All that seemed fine to me because I was still going to South America.)

As a field unit, we were expected to train in the field. That meant jumping from planes carrying full gear, setting up camp, and "snooping and pooping." On one operation we had a captain who did not seem too sharp. He sent three of us, all lieutenants, on a recon mission. We found a highway, flagged down a car, and caught a ride to a corner grocery. There we bought a case of beer and carried it back to camp, where we hid it in a stream. We invited our friends to take a walk with us and sample some of our treasure. By evening I was barely able to talk and was wondering if the captain would suspect anything. Luckily he was not sharp, and nothing ever was said, so I guess in this singular incident, we got away with it.

I also brought a fishing rod and reel along. It was one that was collapsible, and I could fit it in my rucksack. I caught a bass that evening, before I was too drunk to fish, and I cleaned and roasted it over the fire. I had fresh fish while the rest of the group ate C rations.

As the summer wore on, rumors began circulating regarding orders for all of us. We knew that we had to get them soon or we might not have enough time left in our enlistment to serve a year in Vietnam. Finally, in July, they were issued. Bowley and I were on a set with fourteen other second-lieutenant classmates for Vietnam. Brooks was going to Jungle School, his choice, and then joining us in-country.

I went home that evening dreading sharing the news with Cookie. Over a glass of wine, I broke the news and was surprised at how calmly she received it. She explained that she had a sixth-sense belief that we would not be going to South America, so she was not shocked by the orders. I was to report to Oakland, California, for deployment on September 15, 1969, but I was given thirty days for leave and travel. That meant we had time to spend together before my departure.

A place that I had always wanted to go, and that Cookie loved, was Mexico. We decided to spend two weeks of our four touring Mexico with our friends, George and Judy Wimberly. George was a pharmacist who had been able to get out of the draft by taking some drug to raise his blood pressure. He took so much of it that when they drew his blood, it took quite some time to stop the bleeding. George said it looked like they'd punctured an artery.

We drove from Lousiana to Mexico City and then to Acapulco and all the little towns in between. George brought massive amounts of pills along to keep us from getting sick, but he refused to take them. His stubbornness caught up with him just outside Mexico City on the way home. We had adjoining rooms and flipped a coin for the double bed. I was upset that George didn't offer it to me, since I would be leaving in a little over a week, but he didn't, and he won the toss.

The next morning, when he opened his door, I thought I was looking at a ghost. I have never, to this day, seen someone so devoid of color. I discovered that Montezuma had caught him during the night, and he'd spent the entire night with him on the john.

As we headed for Monterrey, our last stop on the way home, I had to pull over several times for George to barf. One time, in a mountain pass, as George was hurling from the backseat, a young Mexican entrepreneur selling beets walked up to George's window, stuck the beets in his face, and asked, "You want?"

George said, "Donnie, grab him. As soon as I finish puking, I want to kill him."

I think the lad understood the sentiment expressed and beat a hasty retreat.

That night, our last in Mexico, we spent in Monterrey. Judy, George's wife, had only one item that she wanted to bring home, paper flowers, but George refused to let her buy any. That last night, as George hovered near death and Judy pestered him relentlessly, he finally gave her the traveler's checks, and then she and Cookie left for the market. The next morning George sat in the backseat surrounded by paper flowers.

As we crossed the border and stopped for lunch, George was so excited to see Men and Ladies on the restroom doors, instead of Hombres and Damas. We arrived home in good spirits, with just a week left of leave before I reported to Oakland. I must say that the prospect of going to Vietnam and leading men in battle was exciting. I had trained for this for over a year, and I felt ready. The thought that I might not come home at all or that I might come home horribly mutilated never entered my mind. That might happen to other people, but not to me.

Cookie, on the other hand, was thinking those thoughts more and more and wondering how we would survive this time apart. Each of us retreated into our own thoughts and tried to keep up appearances.

Finally the morning of September 15, 1969, arrived. I went to the Lafayette airport outfitted in my dress greens, bloused pants tucked into my Corcoran Jump Boots, which were polished to a mirror luster. I had my silver wings on my chest and my green beret on my head. I was ready for war, even if no one else in the family was. As I boarded the plane, I was excited. I would meet Bowley in San Francisco; we would have dinner together and then take a cab to the Oakland depot for travel to the Republic of Vietnam. We just had to be in Oakland by midnight to comply with our orders. The first part of the trip was underway.

# ON THE WAY TO THE REPUBLIC OF VIETNAM

"Lieutenant Bacque, please proceed to the nearest courtesy phone."
I had just landed in San Francisco and was walking through the terminal carrying my duffel bag. I knew Bowley would arrive before me. He had my arrival info, so I was scanning the terminal looking for him. The announcement caused a momentary fear that maybe something had gone wrong already, and I was not even out of the country.

"Lieutenant Bacque here," I spoke into the phone.

"You asshole, where are you?" I heard Bowley mutter. I could tell he had been drinking.

Since I thought I heard an echo, I looked up from the phone, and at the next courtesy phone, just several feet away, I saw Bowley. His tie was undone, one pant leg had lost its blouse and was hanging down, his uniform coat was unbuttoned, and he looked, even from that distance, like hell.

I hung up the phone and started toward him. He was trying to get me back on the line and started banging the phone on the wall. That alarmed me, so I called out. "Bowley, I'm right behind you!" He turned quickly and gave me a smile.

"I've been here a couple of hours, and I've spent all my money at the bar. Not one Mother Fucker offered to buy me a drink. I'm going to Vietnam to die, and no one gives a shit! Ain't that a bitch. Do you have some coins? Let's get a beer."

"Bowley, first you need to start looking better; let's go in the restroom and fix your uniform. Then we can go to the bar. I'll buy you a drink, and we can decide where we will have dinner and then go to Oakland. How does that sound?"

"OK."

We entered the establishment, with Bowley, once again, looking like a Special Forces lieutenant, and we took seats at the bar. The bartender seemed a little hostile at first, but I engaged him in conversation, and he soon warmed up to us, even as Bowley was cursing the fact that I was buying, not the other patrons.

"We get a lot of soldiers through here, heading over, and this is not the friendliest town for them."

*No shit*, I thought.

"Let me ask you this," I said. "If you were us, and this could be your last night in the good old USA, where would you have dinner? We have to report to Oakland by midnight, but until then we are on leave."

I don't remember what he told us, because by then I was drinking, but he wrote down a name and gave it to us. He said the cab driver would know where it was and that the ride there was about an hour. From there to Oakland was another hour, so he told us we needed to leave the restaurant by 10:00 p.m., at the latest, to be sure to make it on time. Then he said, "The drinks are on the house; I wish you well."

As we walked out of the terminal, looking for a cab, I turned to Bowley and said, "They're not all assholes, and I guess he discovered that neither are we."

I really don't remember much about the meal, but I do know we each had steaks as well as prodigious amounts of alcohol. We asked the waiter to get us a cab and tell the driver to take us to the Oakland Replacement Depot. We got in the backseat, and both of us passed out.

"Lieutenants, we're here."

I looked up, and we were outside of a large, brightly lit hangar.

"This is the repo depot."

"Do you have any idea where we go?"

"Report to that little office where the line is." The cab driver pointed to the right.

"How much do we owe you?"

"The ride is on me. Good luck."

I noticed that the meter had not been turned on, so it read zero.

"Look, I really appreciate the offer, but we can afford to pay."

"Lieutenant, don't insult me—the ride is on me."

I shook his hand, as did Bowley, realizing that in the middle of ground zero of the antiwar movement, we had found two kind souls.

"Bowley, with this kind of luck starting out, I bet we both make it home OK."

"Bullshit," he said.

We reported in and were told to go into the hangar where we would be assigned places. The hangar was huge, dimly lighted, and the floor was covered with cots, almost all occupied by soldiers just like us, heading for Vietnam.

"You lieutenants are lucky; you just made it. If you had gotten here past midnight and missed your flight, you would have to pay your own way to Vietnam." I thought he was bullshitting us, but I later found out that one of our classmates, Jack DaCosta, had been late and was charged $225 for the privilege of flying to Vietnam. Jack was later killed in action at a camp near me.

"Your flight is ready to leave. Just go out that door and get on that blue bus. Good luck."

We boarded the plane, which took off at 1:00 a.m. As we lifted off, there was no sound; even the stewardesses were muted in their briefing. I remember looking around and wondering how many on the plane, besides Bowley and me, were going to come home. That is still an unanswered question.

We were racing the sun, heading west, and we landed in Honolulu at 2:00 a.m., their time, to refuel. After an hour, we took off again, heading for Okinawa. I wrote my first postcard home from the plane, telling Cookie we had been flying for twelve hours and it was still dark outside. I was completely disoriented and not sure what the actual date and time were. I had watched a movie, *The Love Bug*, and read several books.

A few hours later, the sun finally brightened the cabin, and we made our approach to Okinawa. After fifteen hours of flying, we were a little more than halfway there. I was starting to think I might die of boredom before I ever arrived. I wondered how they did it in World War II, taking troop ships over. At least they could move around.

When we landed, we were told we would have a crew change and that we would be on the ground for six hours. There was a PX, a bar, and a barbershop available to us to help kill the time. Since I had not shaved for several days, I decided to get a professional shave and start my mustache. I went into the shop, sat down, and proceeded to get butchered by the barber. I had forgotten that army barbers were not necessarily professionally trained. My face oozing blood from the multiple razor cuts, I made a vow to never again get a shave in an army barbershop. But I did have the beginnings of a mustache, and to me, I looked somewhat dashing, in spite of the blood.

At least I could go to the bar and visit with Bowley. Although there were sixteen of us on the same set of orders, all heading for Vietnam, Bowley was the only person I knew on the flight.

After a few beers, a game of pool, and losing ten dollars in the slot machine, it was time to go again.

Next stop: Vietnam.

# VIETNAM

## Thursday, September 18, 1969

As dawn was breaking, the PA system announced that we would soon be approaching the Republic of Vietnam. We had spent almost thirty hours en route, and our anticipation grew as we approached our final destination. We crossed the coast about 9:00 a.m., and then the plane began making evasive maneuvers. No threat was evident, but this was obviously standard procedure. I was sitting at the window and could see fortifications below. Some looked like Special Forces camps or at least what I thought a Special Forces camp should look like. We spiraled into Bien Hoa, arriving at 9:30 a.m. The doors were opened, and the smell of Vietnam greeted us all. The most prominent odor was that of diesel, a smell that to this day brings me back. Although it was just 9:30 a.m. and mid-September, the heat and humidity were oppressive. Even being from Louisiana, I was shocked. As we exited the plane, we could see the people we were replacing, anxiously waiting to board. They were going home and were much more anxious to get on the plane than we felt getting off. There were catcalls and slurs hurled at us, such as "your ass is grass" and "you will probably die, but I didn't," but I was too excited to bother with that. I had spent eighteen months learning how to lead men in battle, and now I was ready to prove that I could.

We were taken to Long Binh, in beautiful air-conditioned buses; I had been expecting a school bus with screened windows. When we arrived, Bowley went to the replacement office and made his call. He had been given a number by a sergeant at Fort Bragg, and he followed those instructions. As I watched him speak, I could see the excitement grow in his face. I listened to the one-sided conversation:

"This is Lieutenant Bowley; we just arrived, and I was told to call this number. Yes, Sergeant Major, there are sixteen of us here now. That's correct; all second lieutenants and all graduates of the Special Forces officer course. Hold on, the replacement-duty NCO is right here."

The sergeant took the phone from Bowley.

"This is the duty NCO. You want them all? You're sending a plane? I'll have them at the airfield at three o'clock tomorrow morning. Thank you, Sergeant Major."

All sixteen of us were going to Special Forces, the best unit in Vietnam. Bowley was our hero.

We drew our gear, had some food, and tried to rest before we departed Long Binh. As the evening sky darkened on my first day in-country, I went to the officers club to meet Brooks. He had just arrived from Jungle School and was excited that all of us had gotten SF, but he was very worried that he wouldn't. While in Jungle School, he had run into our friend Bob Bruce, who was in the class before him. Bruce told him that Jungle School was a piece of cake but to be careful of the ladies of the night, as they had more than commercial affection to give. Bob had just been to the dispensary to be treated for the lagniappe. We didn't know it, but Bob had already died in action—what a waste.

As we sat and reminisced, I reassured Bill that the army could not possibly fight this war without him in SF and bought him a beer. Sitting on the patio, I could see a Douglas AC-47 "Spooky" gunship making a run just on the horizon. Here I was observing a battle while sipping a beer and sitting in the comfort of a bar. How soon would I be out there, having the gunships support me, wishing I were in a bar? What a dichotomy this war was presenting.

I finished my beer, and then went to close my eyes for a few hours. Next stop, Nha Trang. Maybe Brooks would follow.

# NHA TRANG

## Friday, September 19, 1969

We arrived in Nha Trang at 5:00 a.m. and were taken to Special Forces headquarters where, after breakfast, we were placed in an auditorium and briefed as to what to expect. That briefing was done by a master sergeant, who began with an admonition.

"Men, you have just reported to the headquarters of the finest outfit in Vietnam. We have a reputation as the best fighters, the smartest soldiers, and the most professional force in-country. That means that most of you will live to depart. Those who don't, at least you will die being with the best.

"Now, we have never had this many second lieutenants report in before; in fact, you are among the first of many. We are phasing out of Vietnam, and by the time you go home, we probably will have very few SF in-country. For those of you who are unaware of the geography here, there are four corps in Vietnam: I Corps (pronounced "eye corps") is on the DMZ, II Corps (pronounced "two corps") is in the Central Highlands, III Corps (pronounced "three corps") is around Saigon, and IV Corps (pronounced "four corps") is in the Delta. Since there are sixteen of you, four will go to each corps. Raise your hands when I call an area, and the first four of you to do so will go there."

I had talked to different people since I arrived, asking where was the best place to go to lessen my chances of dying. I knew that I Corps was where Khe Sanh was located and was considered to be a "hot" area. III Corps was another supposedly "hot" area, and having grown up in close proximity to rice fields, I decided IV Corps was not to my liking. Using that process of elimination, I raised my hand for II Corps and was chosen, along with Sammy Henderson, Ron Saatoff, and Jack DaCosta. Bowley opted for III Corps and got his choice.

We had our assignments, but first we had to go through a ten-day combat-orientation course, COC, on Hon Tre Island, just offshore of Nha Trang. In my letter to Cookie, written on September 20, I mentioned how beautiful and peaceful Nha Trang seemed:

> If it hadn't been for the barbed wire and armed guards, we could have been in Ft. Bragg. The officers club is much nicer than the club at Bragg, and I am so impressed with the quality of the cadre. No other unit gives you the in-country orientation that we will get, and I know, when we are sent to our final detachment, we will be better prepared than any other junior officer assigned to any other unit.

I also mentioned that we found out that Brooks had been assigned to MACV, the worst possible assignment. So far I had been lucky; would that luck hold?

On Sunday, September 21, we boarded boats and were transported to Hon Tre to begin our ten-day problem. The officers were joined by enlisted men, also recent arrivals, and one of the enlisted was someone I knew at LSU, as well as someone I had gone to high school with—what a small world Vietnam seemed to be. We were assigned to barracks in a little encampment that had both officers and an enlisted club. You could sit on the patio of the officers club and overlook the Nha Trang harbor. The water was a beautiful shade of blue and clear as glass. It reminded me of the Caribbean. Where was this war we were supposed to be fighting? It wasn't around here.

The next day we started our training with a forced march up a trail to the top of a small mountain, carrying a fifty-pound rucksack. Although the climb wasn't easy, by any means, I found out that I was still in shape, despite my month of drinking and partying. Once we finished the hike, we had breakfast and then classroom training on map reading. At noon we were given a two-and-a-half-hour lunch break; then we were back in class until 4:15 p.m. At 5:00 p.m. we did another march up the mountain in one-hundred-degree heat and 100 percent humidity. Then I really started to understand what being in shape meant, and I was not.

When we got back, it was time for chow. After chow, as we returned to the barracks, the heavens opened up with the afternoon monsoon. I thought, since there were no women on the island after 5:00 p.m., why not take an outdoor shower in the rain? I went out in my flip-flops, carrying my washcloth and soap. Soon a dozen others joined me, all cavorting in the rain. I suspect if the VC had been watching, they would consider us all *dinky dao*, "crazy" in Vietnamese. This was a typical day at the COC.

The next week went by quickly, and we were all beginning to feel comfortable in our roles. The training was more of a refresher course but still great information, and it helped to cement what we had learned in the States. The final exercise consisted of us separating into teams and going into the jungle. We were told we might run into VC, so we carried live ammo. I suspect there weren't any VC nearby, but why take a chance? We were alert. We moved out at dusk and had a particular spot on the map we were supposed to move to. I was in charge of finding the spot, and we found it easily. I got some praise from the SF sergeant who was our observer, and then I handed off to the next guy. We were in the field for eighteen uneventful hours and then got orders to rendezvous with a Vietnamese boat, take the boat to another part of the island, and secure a beach. The boat was two hours late, couldn't carry all of us, and let us off on the wrong destination beach. To compound the problem, the water was so shallow that the boat could only come within one hundred yards of the shore, and the beach they offloaded us to was not sand, just mud. Finally we were picked up by a helicopter and brought back to Nha Trang, proud graduates of Special Forces "in-country training."

The next day, October 1, I would report to Pleiku for the next chapter.

# PLEIKU

We flew into Pleiku midmorning and reported to the C-Team orderly room. We were told that we were expected, but the commanding officer (CO) was on R and R, so we would be meeting with the executive officer, Lt. Col. Irizarry. I began to think that there were more lieutenant colonels in Special Forces than lieutenants. I was probably right because although the Fifth Group commanding officer was a full colonel, there was a myriad of lieutenant colonels in his command. Every C-Team had two, every B-Team had one, and the Nha Trang staff seemed to have several dozen. We reported in to Lt. Col. Irizarry, and he immediately focused on me.

"Lieutenant Bacque, you look Spanish, but your name is French."

"My mother is from Puerto Rico, sir."

"Where in Puerto Rico?"

"Caguas, sir."

"I'm from Caguas; what was your mother's maiden name?"

"Aponte, sir."

"I know your family; your grandfather was the postmaster."

"That is correct, sir."

Meanwhile, the other three lieutenants in the room must have been wondering what was going on; they were being completely ignored.

Finally Lt. Col. Irizarry looked at them, asked some perfunctory questions, and then asked us whether we wanted to go to North II Corps or South.

Since there was plenty of action in South and he asked me first, I said north, as did Sammy Henderson. With that, we were on our way to Kontum. But first we had to find a chopper to take us, which was difficult because the weather was atrocious. Besides, Martha Raye was rumored to be coming to the compound for a visit, and we wanted to meet her.

Martha Raye had adopted Special Forces as "her guys" and was continuously visiting. We had been told many Martha Raye stories in Nha Trang, and we wanted to experience her firsthand. So we spent the night and actually visited with Martha Raye—the first time I had met a famous person. She was as kind and approachable as we had been led to believe, and both Sammy and I were able to visit with her, face-to-face, for some time. Between the excitement of meeting her and the cheap booze available to us, the night went by in a blur. Had I not written to Cookie of the evening, I probably would have had no recollection. The next morning, tired and hung over, Sammy and I flew to Kontum, to meet our new commander, Lt. Col. John R. Hennigan.

# KONTUM CITY, REPUBLIC OF VIETNAM

## October 5, 1969

"**B**acque, where are you from?"

"Louisiana, sir."

"Where did you go to school?"

"LSU, sir."

"I'll be damned. I graduated from LSU in 1954, and you are the first junior officer from there whom I have ever commanded. Welcome to Vietnam."

This conversation had started very simply with, "Lieutenant Bacque, sir, reporting for duty."

I was addressing Lt. Col. John Hennigan, Infantry, Airborne, and commander of the Special Forces B-Team, located in Kontum, Republic of South Vietnam. Col. Hennigan was a big man; he seemed to be in his late thirties to early forties, with a graying flattop. He smoked a cigarette as he sat behind his desk, very comfortable in his surroundings. His voice had the raspy quality that most longtime smokers have, and he actually reminded me a little of John Wayne. He had two files in front of him; one must have been mine. Sammy Henderson, standing at attention beside me, and I were his two new replacements, and it was easy to see that he was wondering what to do with us. Sammy was from Texas, so Col. Hennigan seemed less interested in him than me.

"Bacque, I know you're here to kill commies for Christ, but I don't have a combat post to send you to. I'm going to send you to a camp that hasn't heard an enemy shot fired in twelve months; Henderson, you will be going to one just as quiet. Visit with the sergeant major to get your instructions."

If he thought that I would be disappointed, he was wrong. I had made a conscious decision not to die in Vietnam, and this was a good start.

He dismissed us before adding, "Oh, by the way, I don't like facial hair."

Both Sammy and I had grown what we considered to be stylish mustaches while going through our in-country combat orientation.

"Sir," I said, "I was planning to shave it today."

"Good boy."

The look Sammy gave me was sufficient: "What a kiss-up." But what the hell—the colonel held my life in his hands.

As we walked down the hall, I turned to Sammy.

"Where do you think we are going?"

"He really didn't say, but it didn't sound bad. I guess the sergeant major will have the scoop. Do you think we should find him now?"

"I prefer sooner rather than later," I replied. "Let's go now."

We knocked on the sergeant major's office door and waited until he called us in.

He stood as we walked in and saluted us. I was still not completely comfortable with being saluted by a person who had served for over twenty years and was old enough to be my father. The sergeant major was smaller than the colonel but still commanded respect. He had sandy hair and a funny way of expressing himself. It was as if his gestures were a few beats later than his words, which I found a little disconcerting.

"Colonel says you are the fresh meat. Did he tell you where you are headed?"

"No, Sergeant Major," I answered, "but he did say that neither one of us was going to someplace hot."

"Lieutenant, do you know where you are? Vietnam is hotter than hell."

"I meant a place where there was action."

Then he smiled knowingly and said, "You are going to Dak Pek, and Lieutenant Henderson to Dak Seang. Good luck; you will need it."

He saluted, letting us know the visit was over, and Sammy and I left.

"I wonder what he meant by all that," Sammy said. "The colonel must know more than him, and he said we were going on vacation."

"Sammy, let's believe the colonel; I think the sergeant major is playing with us."

"Well, one of them is."

We drew our gear and were told to be ready to fly out the next morning. Since Sammy was going to be just south of me, we would fly out together, and he'd be dropped off first. That night we ate dinner and then went to the officers club, an eight-by-ten closet with every bottle of booze you could think of. There was a Montagnard bartender; country music playing in the background; a poker table, where I saw Martha Raye take almost every penny an unsuspecting major had (but that's another story); and three tables where we could sit, drink, and visit.

After a few beers, I was ready to quit. I looked at my watch to check the time.

"It can't be that late. What time is it?" Sammy said. "I lost my watch during orientation and haven't had a chance to replace it. I was hoping to get a Mickey Mouse (an army-issue plastic watch). Doesn't look like that will happen. Hope I don't need one soon."

"It's eleven. I'm tired, and I think I'll turn in."

With that I bade Sammy good night and went to my temporary quarters.

The next morning we had an early breakfast, reported to the helipad, and boarded our chopper. On the chopper, in addition to us, were two veterinarians, headed for Dak Pek. I thought that was strange and asked them why they were headed there. They replied that the army was concerned that the numerous dogs owned by the Montagnards (the mountain people indigenous to the Central Highlands of Vietnam) posed a rabies danger, so the vets were going out to vaccinate the dogs. The flight to Dak Seang usually took thirty to forty minutes, depending on whether we stopped in Dak To. Today it was a straight shot. We landed, Sammy got off, and we took off again for Dak Pek. The day was overcast and dreary, and it actually was cold in the cabin because we flew with the doors open. I could see the jungle below us, and I was amazed at how unspoiled it seemed. Around the camps and firebases, there was an ugly, red scar carved in the ground that was dusty in the dry season and thick mud in the monsoon season, but the jungle seemed untouched. I couldn't help but wonder what was down there beneath the beautiful green canopy; guess I'd find out soon enough.

Then I noticed a change of pitch, and I could make out a camp in the distance. The door gunner tapped me on the shoulder and mouthed "Dak Pek" as he pointed. Dak Pek was the most northern camp in II Corps, located just south of I Corps and just a few miles east of the Laotian border. It had been constructed in this location in 1964 because it was astride a major infiltration route from the Ho Chi Minh trail, which ran just on the other side of the border.

The camp appeared on a high hill, surrounded by smaller hills. I could see a runway and a helicopter landing pad, where a smoke grenade was showing us the wind direction. Suddenly the copter started jigging, and I was thrown off balance. I was strapped in, with no danger of falling out, but the movement both surprised and concerned me. It was over as quickly as it occurred, and we landed. After I gathered my gear, I went to the pilot's window and asked him what happened.

"We took fire coming in and took a few hits. Nothing serious, just part of the daily routine," he replied.

Maybe Col. Hennigan knew more than he told me.

"Hey Lieutenant, I'm Captain Kazanowski, the camp CO. Welcome aboard."

I had seen the captain walking down to greet us. I saluted and told him that I was happy to be here.

"No saluting here; we can shake hands," he said. "You got a little welcoming reception that we did not intend. We had a Caribou (a resupply aircraft) also take fire today. Something is going on, so I'm taking a patrol out tomorrow to check it out. I want you to visit with Lieutenant O, the CAPO officer, and learn what he is doing; you'll be taking over from him."

I went to the team hut, a multiuse wooden building, and met O. He looked and acted like a clown, with rumpled fatigues, muddy boots, and an overall disheveled look that the other team members did not possess. I remember wondering how he had qualified for Special Forces and how he had remained alive to date. That conversation would eventually be had, but for now I was left to speculate.

The team hut and all the living quarters were underground, which provided a natural cooling effect. In the team room were a card table, a Ping-Pong table, a stereo, a movie screen, a bar with free booze, and a TV. War is hell!

All of the food and drinks were free. The team got free beer and sold what they didn't drink to the Vietnamese and Montagnards. The profits realized from the sales were used to buy our food and pay the mama-sans to wash our uniforms and shine our shoes, and any excess went into a team pot, which was used to help the team members pay for R and R expenses. So much for the "rough life" of a Special Forces soldier, I thought.

My first assignment was to accompany O and the vets as they went from village to village, catching and vaccinating the dogs. O whispered to me, "The yards think this is hilarious, since they are raising the dogs for food."

"Crazy Americans" was their attitude. As the sun was setting, we went back to the camp perimeter.

After a tour around the camp, meeting the other team members, and a great dinner, I retired to O's area, which consisted of a room dug into the hillside completely covered with sandbags and mud. The humidity was near fog level, and the air was chilly. A dehumidifier was going full blast, and O told me that he had to empty it several times a day. There were several beds with mosquito nets attached, so I climbed between damp sheets and wondered what the next day would bring.

It turned out it would not be a good day.

The morning was beautiful, a welcome change, and I remember thinking how bright and clear the sky was as Lt. O and I went to the team hut for breakfast. The team members seemed to readily accept me into their circle, and I thought that my stay here would be pleasant. Besides Capt. Kazanowski and Lt. O, there was a First Lt. Dave Cook who served as the executive officer. Both he and Kazanowski had all the Special Forces traits O seemed to lack, and that made me feel much better. I was excited, looking forward to my first day in camp. Capt. Kazanowski greeted me and told me he would be leaving on a patrol with SFC Lopez after breakfast. My task, he told me, was to visit the Montagnard villages that surrounded the camp and meet the village chieftains. Those villages supplied the several hundred indigenous troops that called Dak Pek home, and we constantly needed new recruits. One of my jobs as CAPO officer would be to replenish the troops we lost due to both WIA (wounded in action) and KIA (killed in action).

O and I got in one of the camp jeeps and started our task about 9:00 a.m. That was when Capt. Kazanowski and his patrol left the camp perimeter. Shortly thereafter, O and I drove up to the first village to meet the chief. The villages consisted of wooden homes, elevated about five to six feet above the ground, and gathered around the chief's house, which was always located in the middle. Each village had a wooden perimeter wall, offering some privacy, but no real defensive security.

As I was introduced to the first chief, he invited me to take a seat in front of a wooden jar. I looked at O and could see him smiling, so I was immediately wary.

"What's going on?" I asked.

"Oh, part of the welcoming of strangers involves drinking rice wine with the chief; you cannot refuse."

Being LSU alum and having some acquaintance with alcohol, I was not unduly concerned, so I asked what was expected.

O said, "Just do what he does."

I noticed that across the lip of the jar, there was a stick, with a peg sticking down into the liquid. A long bamboo straw seemed to reach to the bottom of the jar. The chief sat beside me, took the straw, and drank a long swallow. I could see the liquid move below the peg.

"That is one stick," O said. "You need to drink at least one to be mannerly."

A pitcher of liquid was poured into the jug to bring the level back to the top of the jar.

Certainly not wanting to insult my host, I tentatively took the straw and took a large swallow. I have never, to this day, tasted anything so vile. As I tried not to show my displeasure, O said, "That was half a stick—you need at least one."

I summoned up all my courage and swallowed down one more. The chief, a small, weathered, brown-skinned man who looked like an American Indian, smiled broadly, showing a mouthful of gold teeth. He patted me on the back and shook hands with O. I found myself a little light-headed and wondered why O didn't drink.

"Why aren't you drinking this crap?" I asked when we got back in the jeep.

"I'm driving," he said, and I let the issue drop.

We drove to the next village, where the same ritual was replayed, but this time the drink didn't seem quite as vile, and I was a little more light-headed.

"How many more?" I asked.

"Well, there are seven villages, but we won't be able to get to all of them today. Let's do one more and then go back to the camp for lunch. You're doing fine; I think they like you. In fact, you look a little like them. They may think you are related."

For some reason that was one of the funniest things I had ever heard, and I started laughing hysterically. I was also having trouble sitting in the jeep on the steep and curvy roads. One more, I thought; I'm already blasted.

The last stop was a blur to me, but I do recall O saying we were on our way back to the camp. I remember thinking that I hoped I could stay in the jeep for the trip back. My stomach was sour, and I prayed I wouldn't get sick. Even LSU parties had not prepared me for this.

When we reached the camp, I wondered why all the team members were waiting outside. Then O said, "He did better than most; he hasn't gotten sick yet."

That was something to be proud of.

I staggered into the TOC (tactical operations center), which served as the team room, dining area, and also the radio room, and sat down to lunch.

Suddenly I could hear small-arms fire, and the radio came to life.

"Dak Pek, this is Kilo 2. We are in heavy contact and need fire support."

This was Sgt. Lopez calling for help. He went on. "Kilo 1 [Kazanowski] is down at the head of the column, and I will make my way there to check on him, but I need fire support right now."

He gave his position and signed off.

All this happened in an instant, and before I knew it, the weapons sergeant said, "Lieutenant, get in the mortar pit and drop the rounds while I adjust."

The rest of the team set about assembling a rescue party in case it was needed.

I had fired mortars before, in training, but I had never done it while completely inebriated. The mortar was called a Four Deuce, which meant it was big. The rounds made a tremendous noise when they were fired, and I was very close to the sound. I would never recommend this to anyone, but it did sober me up fast. After we fired a dozen or so rounds, Sgt. Lopez came on the radio.

"I have Kilo 1, and he's KIA. I am coming back in with his body. We are still in heavy contact; can you get us some TAC air support?"

The rescue party started out of the wire, we continued to fire the mortar, and before long aircraft were on-site and making strafing runs. As night started to fall, I could see orange tracers (ours) going out and green tracers (theirs) coming in. As the column made its way back into the camp, the firing stopped and a silence enveloped us. I looked up and saw Col. Hennigan standing there. *Where did he come from?* I wondered. I didn't remember a chopper coming in. Was this what combat was like—you only remember snippets?

"Well, Bacque, how did you like your first day at Dak Pek?" he asked.

"Honestly, sir, I've had better."

"Don't worry, you did fine, but I need you to help gather the captain's possessions so we can ship them home."

Who was this guy? I had just met him yesterday, and now he was dead.

I was about to find out.

The next morning was overcast with intermittent rain and fog, a complete change from the day before. Col. Hennigan spoke to me after breakfast. "I need you to go through the captain's possessions. Do a complete inventory, and make sure there is nothing in them that would embarrass his family. If you have any doubt about anything you find, destroy it. When you have finished, take the first chopper into Pleiku, deliver his belongings to graves registration, and then go back to Kontum and wait for me. I need to stay here a few days, and if anyone asks you what you are doing there, just tell them the colonel has a job for you. That's all you, or they, need to know."

I went to the captain's quarters, feeling like I was violating his privacy. It seems crazy, but all I could think about was the old adage: always wear clean underwear in case you are in an accident. I was hoping all of his were clean.

The captain's room was small but very neat. He had a bed and a bedside table, and on the table was a photograph of Capt. Kazanowski and his bride getting ready to board a helicopter. The caption stated that it was the first leg of their honeymoon. I imagined that this guy, his wife, or both came from money. There was a footlocker at the end of the bed; it was unlocked. That was good, but I had been told to break any locks I found if I needed to. On the footlocker was the web gear that he was wearing when he was shot. I had heard that he was shot in the chest, and I looked to see if there was any blood on the gear. There wasn't. I remember thinking, "How morbid of me." An army-issue Mickey Mouse watch was strapped to the gear. I knew that the captain had no more need for the watch, and Sammy Henderson was probably still looking for one, so I took the watch for Sammy and did not include it in the inventory. The army would consider it to be a combat loss, and I was learning the art of scrounging.

I went through the footlocker and found several newspaper clippings describing the wedding and honeymoon. Another article mentioned that Capt. Kazanowski was a member of the army reserves and had volunteered for combat duty. He did not need to be in Vietnam, but obviously felt it was his duty to go. As I looked at the picture of him and his wife, so alive on that wedding day, I wondered how she would take the terrible news, knowing that a choice, not an order, had brought him to Dak Pek. As I continued the inventory, I got the sense that this person, just a few years older than me, had his life together. Everything was neat, in its place, and nothing of any impropriety was anywhere to be found. I had a personal feeling of regret that I would never get to know more about him. I was sure he would have been an interesting person.

As I finished the inventory and brought his possessions to the team house, I could see that fog was moving in. The radio was on, and I could hear communications between a FAC "bird dog" and the camp. The bird dog was searching for the NVA that had ambushed the patrol the day before, and riding in the backseat was Sgt. Lopez, who had been on the operation. He thought he might be able to pinpoint the enemy location and then call in artillery and TAC air. The pilot radioed that they had been enveloped in a fogbank between their location and Dak Pek. The plane was not equipped for instrument flying, so he was trying to find a path back to camp.

Lt. Cook was in the room and mentioned to me that he was supposed to be on the plane, but he had been stopped on the runway and asked to return to camp, so Sgt. Lopez could take his place. Suddenly the radio went dead, and all attempts to contact the plane were futile. It appeared that they might have crashed, but no one knew where. Lt. Cook was white as a sheet. He knew he had dodged another round.

There was a homing beacon on the plane, so when the weather cleared enough, several planes and helicopters joined the search, all to no avail. The plane had vanished. Since all aircraft were being used in the search, I was still at Dak Pek, waiting for a ride to Pleiku. I spent the next two days waiting around. By then it was obvious that the plane was down and survival was iffy at best for the two occupants. During the search another plane had flown into a mountain, killing another pilot. Because the weather conditions were so inconsistent, a decision was made to terminate the search and just declare the occupants MIA (missing in action). Since I was still at Dak Pek and had experience with inventorying the captain's belongings, I was nominated to do the same for Sgt. Lopez. There was a marked difference in the condition and content of the sergeant's room, not as neat and orderly, but I finished my task after a few hours. That afternoon the weather cleared, and I was able to fly to Kontum.

I still needed to get to Pleiku, but I was told to just take a jeep and drive over. Pleiku was about thirty miles south of Kontum, and a two-lane semi-blacktop road connected the two towns. The shoulder had been cleared to a distance of fifty to seventy-five yards from the road on either side, to help prevent ambushes. There were no houses or businesses along the road from just outside Kontum to just outside Pleiku. If there was trouble, we were on our own. The road passed through a series of small mountains and passes, and would have been quite beautiful if I could have enjoyed the scenery. I traveled with a sergeant, both of us heavily armed, as there was still danger on the road. The trip took about an hour and was uneventful.

In Pleiku I found graves registration, which was the morgue for II Corps. It was located in a large Quonset hut, and the inside was brightly lit and very clean. I didn't know what to expect, maybe a place filled with blood and gore, but that was not the case. I delivered the cataloged contents of the two men's possessions and then proceeded to the C-Team, where I found Sammy. I was happy to see him, and he me. He was like a kid at Christmas when I gave him the watch. I told him the story, in case he was superstitious, but he said the captain's bad luck was his good fortune, and he was happy with the watch. It was getting late in the day, and I had another hour of driving ahead of me, so I started back to Kontum. I remember looking at the setting sun lighting up the clouds. One of the true dichotomies of the country was the sheer beauty of the land countered with the horrible reality of war. I had been in-country for less than a month and was already wondering if I would make it home.

Eleven months to go.

# FUN OFFICER

When I got back to Kontum that evening, rumors were flying. Capt. Gray, a West Point grad, had been sent to Dak Pek as the new camp commander, and the gossip mill was in full swing.

"Bacque, why are you back here?" asked Capt. Galloway, sitting at his desk. He was the S-1, the admin officer.

"Colonel Hennigan told me to come back, but he didn't say why."

"Well, he probably wants you to be the new S-1 and take my place," he said as he played with his paperclips.

"I have no idea; he told me I would find out when he got back."

"OK."

The next day, as we entered the breakfast area, it started again.

"Bacque, you are not going to be the S-1, maybe the assistant S-3." The S-3 was the operations officer.

"I have no idea, but the colonel will let me know."

That afternoon: "Well, it won't be assistant S-3."

"I never said it was."

That went on for several days until Col. Hennigan returned and called me into his office. Sgt. Maj. Campbell was there as well.

I marched in and saluted. "Lieutenant Bacque reporting as ordered."

"At ease," he said. "Well, Bacque, are you ready to find out what your new job will be?"

"Yes, sir, I am."

"Do you know what our mission is in Vietnam?"

"Honestly, sir, no one has shared that with me."

"Well, our mission is to recruit, train, and lead in battle—indigenous personnel."

"Yes, sir," I said, wondering exactly what that had to do with my new position.

"The job I am giving you has great danger as well as responsibility. The Vietnamese will try to subvert you, offering you money, women, drugs, and alcohol."

As my mind was racing, all I could think was, *Obviously he wants an LSU alum, who would be used to debauchery, to have this job.*

He went on. "I want you to be my funds officer"—but I heard "fun officer." I was already confused by the pampered lifestyle of the Special Forces personnel I had met, compared with a regular army unit, and wondered how a fun officer might fit into the command structure.

The colonel interrupted my reverie as he proceeded.

"We recruit and train the local Montagnards as well as pay them. We are funded through the CIA, and your job will be to draw funds monthly, distribute those funds to the camps, and account for them when the payroll is completed. How did you do in accounting?"

"Not very well, sir."

"Well, can you add and subtract, and keep your checkbook balanced?"

"Yes, sir, I am OK with that."

"Then you'll do fine. Go find Lieutenant Light and tell him you are his replacement. Also, while you are training with him, I want you to be the interim club officer. I had to send Captain Gray to Dak Pek, and I do not have a replacement. You can do that as well."

"Yes, sir."

I saluted and left with my mind spinning. Funds officer, club officer, and I had barely gotten through Accounting 101. I had heard the phrase "close enough for government work" and wondered if it applied here.

When I reported in to Lt. Melvin D. Light and announced I would be his replacement, he seemed upset. I did not know it at the time, but a captain had extended for six months and had expected to be appointed the funds officer when Mel left. Here I was, a new second lieutenant taking the job the captain was expecting. Lt. Light knew this, even though I didn't—the reason for his displeasure.

I later deduced that Col. Hennigan actually wanted Capt. Gray to be the funds officer, but when he had to send the captain to Dak Pek, his plans changed. The colonel was also concerned, because of the very loose controls in place, that someone could easily divert funds to his own benefit. Col. Hennigan divulged this to me several months later over a beer and told me that when the captain had volunteered for the position, he became suspicious. He thought that since I was a Louisiana boy, as well as an LSU grad, I probably didn't know enough to get in trouble. He was right.

# CLUB OFFICER

**M**y new job training consisted of watching Mel do his job, which took four to six days a month. With plenty of free time on my hands, I started looking into the club operation. Capt. Gray had been gone for several weeks, and during that time there was no real supervision. The first night when I closed the clubs, both officer and enlisted, I found a shortage of $140. I checked and rechecked my figures, and I could not find the missing funds. I reported it to the colonel the next day, and he told me not to worry, but to make sure it never happened again. I decided since it must have happened in the interim, the colonel knew I was not responsible, but he also wanted me to know that he expected all books to balance. I took his advice seriously.

As I researched the club history, I found out that the club had been running a $40,000 deficit just six months back, and now had a $56,000 profit. This was occurring at the same time as a major scandal involving a Sgt. Major Woolrich, in which he was accused of skimming hundreds of thousands of dollars from enlisted clubs. Well, if our club, which sold beer for twenty cents and mixed drinks for twenty-five cents, could move from a $40,000 deficit to a $56,000 profit in six months, there was no doubt of both the profit potential and the amount of booze that our soldiers consumed.

I also found a special fund called the "Charity Fund." No one seemed to know much about it, but I found a staff sergeant who said he thought the fund was the result of a dice table that used to run at B-24. Supposedly the profits from the table were running $2,000 to $4,000 per week. Somehow word got back to headquarters regarding this game, and they said to shut it down. By the time that happened, there was a sizable amount of profit and no place to put it, so a charity fund was set up. Those monies were then used to buy anything that members of B-24 needed: food for the mess hall, soft drinks and mugs for the officers, as well as clothes and construction material for the local orphanage. Not all expenses could qualify as charity, but no one seemed to care.

The biggest problem for me was that I was now working every day from 6:00 a.m. until the bars closed, and that happened when the last person left. One night the colonel decided to stay until 1:30 p.m., and when Martha Raye was in camp, the bar closed when the card game ended.

One other duty of the club officer was booking floor shows into Kontum. Many bands toured the Vietnam circuit. Most were Filipino, but a few were Australian. The men much preferred the Australian shows, but they were happy with any group that included women. I not only had to book the shows but find accommodations for the performers, as we could not allow them to stay in our compound overnight. Col. Hennigan did not want any women on base, and that upset some of the guys who had "live-in" mama-sans before he arrived.

The first show I booked had a nine-year-old lead singer, who was supposed to be great. I would not know, because I was the duty officer the night of the show, so I missed it. But I had some excitement anyway. That was the night the Mets won the World Series, and I remember trying to find a radio so I could hear the game, but to no avail. (I did write Cookie the next day, telling her that if the Mets won, next LSU would be number one, and the Saints would win the Super Bowl. How long did that take?)

As duty officer, my job was to supervise the tactical operations center with a duty NCO. We would remain awake all night long, periodically inspecting the perimeter, and waking the camp if anything dangerous occurred. That morning, around 2:00 a.m. or 3:00 a.m., after the floor show had packed up and left, I heard some explosions. I turned to the duty NCO and asked him, "Is that incoming?"

"I'm not sure, Lieutenant; I'm new in-country, but it does sound like incoming."

"What do you think we should do? I hate to sound the alarm for no good reason."

As the NCO shrugged his shoulders, I saw Sgt. Maj. Campbell come running into the TOC, a .45 in his hand, his flack vest hanging from one arm, and a steel pot on his head.

"You dumb SOBs, that's incoming! Sound the alarm! Make sure everyone gets to their assigned positions, and be careful getting to yours—they may be in the wire."

I can tell you that going to my assigned bunker was a challenge, as I was wondering if every shadow I saw was an NVA, planning to do me harm. I finally arrived, in good health, just as the all clear sounded. It seems that the VC had attacked the airstrip with mortars, damaged a few helicopters, and then disappeared. This became a routine occurrence, and by the end of my tour, I knew what incoming sounded like, but by then I had developed nonchalance to hearing it.

# MARTHA RAYE

Through the years, the legend of Martha Raye has grown, but I can tell you that nothing said about her has been magnified. She was the "real thing." Each time I saw her, which was often, she was wearing jungle fatigues, the caduceus of the medical corps, jump wings, a lieutenant colonel's rank on her collar, and a green beret. I have no idea if any of this was actually earned, except for the caduceus, as she was said to be a real nurse, but she wore it all with such authority that I am sure no one had the temerity to question her. She exuded command presence and was very comfortable in our surroundings. I am not sure if she ever actually went back to the States. In my year in Kontum, I saw her at least quarterly, so I suspect she just stayed. She would arrive, most of the time unannounced, on a helicopter that she probably commandeered. She respected all authority but gave not an inch if she felt that the command given her was wrong. I would not want to be the object of her wrath, as she had no one but herself to answer to. She loved Special Forces, and we loved her. But her real love and her forte was poker, and she was a formidable player. But that is another story.

In fact, she was so well liked by the officers and men of B-24 that Col. Hennigan ordered me to get a plaque made for her that said,

"The only thing bigger than your heart is your smile."
From the officers and men of B-24

In order to get it made, I had to go to the central market in Kontum. The market offered any item of clothing, gear, or food we could think of. Most of the items for sale were made in the United States and pilfered from the docks in Saigon and Cam Ranh Bay. Items that were difficult for us to get through normal channels were all on display and for sale in the market. There was even an engraving booth, and that's where I got the plaque made.

The market reminded me of some I had experienced in Mexico. The most dominant feature was the smell. The odors of dead chickens being scalded and plucked merged with the scent of beef that had been butchered several days ago. And then there was the aroma of fish, as well as the ever-present Nuoc Mam a rancid fish sauce used as a condiment on all Vietnamese dishes. If you did not have a strong stomach, you could easily get sick. Despite the stench, the noise, the crowd, and the confusion, I was able to complete my task and return with the memento to B-24.

## Kontum Market

Now that we had it, we just had to arrange to give it to her. But since her visits were relatively often, I knew that we would not have to wait long.

# THE XO

The B-24 executive officer (XO) was a major who, in the chain of command, was just under Col. Hennigan. I found him fascinating, almost a caricature of a Special Forces soldier. He was slender, good looking, and very put together in appearance. He never went anywhere without a SOG knife on his belt in a scabbard made from monkey skin. Supposedly he got it when he served in Laos with the Meo tribesmen. The only problem, or at least one of them, was he seemed to walk around mumbling to himself, almost like he was continually on drugs or hung over from alcohol. I never saw him appear completely unaffected.

One day during the staff briefing, as Col. Hennigan was talking to him, the major was picking lint off of his uniform, seemingly not paying any attention to what was being said. I suspect if he had not been "short"—he had less than a month left in-country—Col. Hennigan would have asked for a replacement.

He did excel at one task, and that was playing poker. It wasn't so much that he was skilled, he just had more money than most of us, and he would "buy" pots by raising the ante so much that no one could afford to call him. Because I was still the club officer and had to stay until closing, I saw many of his card games.

The best, though, was when Martha Raye finally arrived to pick up her plaque. She was truly touched by our memento and gave a wonderful talk to all of us. Then she retired to the club and the poker table. The major was one of the participants. Late in the evening, he began his raises, matched dollar for dollar by Martha Raye. I suspect she had played cards with him before and knew what to expect. I am not sure how much was in the pot, or what the last raise the major made was, but she called.

"You can't bluff me, and you can't win this hand. I could take every penny you have, but I won't. Show me your cards, and then I am going to bed" she said confidently.

Needless to say, she won, and the major slunk off to bed as well.

A few days later, we were in the mess hall, and Lt. Light was talking about playing chess. The major said that he would really like to learn the finer points of the game because he wanted to play with a lieutenant who was out of the country at that time. Lt. Light told me later that the lieutenant was a chess hustler, letting you win the first game and then playing you for money after. Obviously he had clipped the major for a few bills, and the major wanted to get them back. I guess he thought he could master the game with an hour or so of instruction from Mel.

Then he went on to tell us that he thought it was awful of that lieutenant to take advantage of people like him.

"There doesn't seem to be any honor anymore. For the lieutenant to take advantage of me like he did is just not proper. I wonder what this world is coming to. I would never stoop to that level."

Later, in the club, after a few drinks, he told us that once he had won eighty-five dollars from a young lieutenant, playing horseshoes. I almost choked on my drink because I was laughing so hard. I told Cookie in my letter that day, "I'm kind of sorry he is leaving; I think he is funny as hell."

One of my other tasks during this time period was serving as MPC exchange officer. We were not allowed to have American dollars in Vietnam; we had to use MPCs, military payment certificates. The bills kind of looked like Monopoly money, but we could use them to buy anything we wanted. We were not supposed to use them in the local economy, but everyone did. So, every so often, there was an exchange, where we had to turn in our old MPC and get a new issue. All the bases were locked down, so no civilians could get their MPC changed, and what they held would be worthless the next day. Supposedly, whenever this happened, the army would make several million dollars. But plenty of troops accommodated their Vietnamese friends and changed their money, even though it was against regulations. I was in charge of B-24 and all the camps. I was issued a lot of new MPC and exchanged with all the men. The major saw what I was doing and came up.

"Lieutenant Bacque, could you souvenir me some extra money out of that bundle?" The Vietnamese would use the word "souvenir" as a verb, instead of "give."

"I'll tell you what, Major; I don't have any to souvenir you, but why don't we play a game of chess? Who knows, you might win."

He left, obviously upset with my flippancy.

Later that evening he took me aside. "You don't realize this now, but when I'm gone, you will miss me. I think you have potential in this army, and when I leave, you will no longer have my guidance, leadership, or example to follow."

He was serious as hell, and it was all I could do to keep from laughing out loud.

The next day he tried to get a chopper pilot to let him fly the bird. Since I was on the helicopter at the time, his request raised my level of concern. He explained to me, after the pilot refused his request, that he didn't need to go to flight school; he was already expert in flying. I would let him prove that to someone else.

Later I found out that he could fly a helicopter; he was actually flying one from Ben Het to Kontum, but he had to crash-land due to a mechanical failure. Luckily I was not aboard, and none of the occupants were injured.

Finally his farewell arrived. That afternoon, he was trying to get someone to play him in Ping-Pong, for money, of course. He got no takers. All that night he bought the bar, and the next morning, bleary eyed but otherwise no different, he bade us good-bye, heading for Germany, an unforgettable character until the end.

I heard later that while he was in Germany, he was subject to a RIF (reduction in force) to the rank of sergeant. This supposedly happened because he had been caught with a senior officer's wife. I have no idea if this was true, but it would not have surprised me if it were.

# MY JOB

Finally, on October 20, I took over as the funds officer, and at almost the same time, Lt. Brown replaced me as club officer. Now I could concentrate on my real job. Mel was still in the compound, but he had less than a month left in-country, so he mentored me while I performed the actual task. My monthly routine consisted of going to the Pleiku C-Team, picking up and signing for the money—approximately five million piastres every month—and then breaking the money down for each camp, based on the payroll sheets. I would then deliver the funds to the camps, and after the camp indigenous personnel were paid, I would return to pick up payroll sheets and leftover funds.

Back at B-24, I would reconcile the numbers and bring the excess funds and the original payroll sheets to Pleiku. The mechanics of the operation took only five to seven days per month, and for the remainder of the month, I had little or nothing to do. My direct superior was Col. Hennigan, so I was almost out of the chain of command. If he wanted me to do something more, he would ask; if not, no one told me what to do. Not bad duty. But when I did work, it was twelve to eighteen hours per day. I guess you could say we condensed a month's work into seven days. I had a support staff of four civilians, including my bodyguard/interpreter, Jolys; a Vietnamese accountant, Mr. Nahn; and two secretaries to help with the paperwork. I also had a private office—the only other private offices belonged to the colonel and Maj. Ramos.

On October 23, I drove the thirty miles to Pleiku with Jolys and picked up my first payroll. The piastres were packaged in bundles tied with string, about the size of a large brick. Each bundle supposedly contained one hundred b, Lieutenant. I knew I could count on you."

I saluted and left, wondering what my accounting professor
hought of my solution. Based on my grades, I suspect he would
1 either surprised or proud. But I was pleasing the colonel, and
e important.

's later I was audited.

n't know how this would affect other people, but the fact that I
dited did cause me some angst. I had to leave my office and wait
lled back. The auditor was a first lieutenant, about my age, but
1 done better in accounting than I did.

e called me in.

ant, what did you do?"

sure I understand the question," I replied, my heart beating

anced. How did you do that?"

an LSU grad, but I was smart enough to know that this question
ve a direct answer.

ask you this—is balancing good or bad?"

f course it's good, but no one balances."

onel told me that this was simple addition and subtraction, just
ng account. You draw money, you pay, and then what is left should
ng balance."

:orrect."

e I balance, I did a good job?"

correct. Congratulations."

e left, I could tell he was still wondering how I did it.

t month I was five hundred piastres under, so I took that amount
perty safe, transferred it to the audit safe, and once again balanced.
:ks later, the same auditor showed up again for an unannounced
ice again was amazed at my pristine books.

to the colonel, with me in tow, and announced to Col. Hennigan
g:

thousand piastres, so I would get fifty bun
count the bills, so I just counted the bu
sack, hefted it over my shoulder, and carri
the jeep. I know I must have looked some
in green and having no facial hair. Then J
where I broke the bills down, still wrapped
our camps over a two-day time period. Th
A-Camps, from north to south: Dak Pek,
and to the northeast, Plateau Gi, the only

We also had Mang Buk, north of Plat
the Vietnamese in December. Although I co
Mang Buk was turned over, I was never rec
told why, and I never asked.

The camp executive officers, or their de
ant on-site, would pay the troops, have the
their excess funds and the payroll sheet to
monies that had been paid out, subtract tha
just like you do with your checking account

The only problem was that it didn't. A
one thousand piastres left over, about one h
considering I picked up five million, but I r
me after the $140 mishap at the club: "I e
enough for government work" for him.

I went through the entire payroll a secor
was very concerned, and then I thought, "Y
is a lot. Since the bills were counted by hand
mistake. If it is in my favor this time, maybe

So I decided to create my own "funds of
safes: one an audit safe, subject to random a
could store valuables for team members. The
audit, and the auditor was not allowed to ch
sand piastres and put them in the property sa
that to Col. Hennigan.

"Good
Beamir
would have
not have be
that was m

Two we
Now I
was being a
until I was
obviously h

Finally
"Lieute
"I'm ne
rapidly.
"You ba
I may b
did not des
"Let m
"Well,
"The c
like a check
be your ene
"That's
"So, sir
"That
But as
The ne
from the p

Two w
audit and c

He wer
the followi

"Sir, I am not sure how this lieutenant is doing what he is doing, but he is by far the best funds officer I've seen, and I've seen them all. Would you mind if during his down time, we sent him around the country to teach other funds officers how to keep the books?"

Now Col. Hennigan was beaming as he said, "That shouldn't be a problem, but I don't want you working him too hard."

So it came to pass that on my twenty or so days when I had nothing to do, I would get on a helicopter and ride. And wherever it landed, I would ask the funds officer, "Do you have two safes?"

And then I'd reveal my secret, with an admonition that the secret had to be kept between us.

The colonel was happy, the other funds officers were happy, the auditors were happy, and my life was great. I was a hero, just because the colonel had made me figure out how to make sure I balanced. I guess he knew that a Louisiana boy could find an angle.

This may also have saved my life, because a typical lieutenant's assignment was six months of admin and then six months in the field, usually in reverse order, the field first. After six months as the funds officer, Col. Hennigan called me into his office.

"Lieutenant Bacque, you have been here six months, and I have orders assigning you to Dak Seang. I know you are anxious to go"—I really wasn't—"but you are too valuable to me and our mission. I can't afford to let you go, so I am sending Lieutenant Christianson in your place."

Two months later Dak Seang was hit by the NVA, and Lt. Christianson was seriously wounded.

And so it was that my entire tour of duty was spent in B-24 keeping the books balanced. And though I was subject to ambush on my many trips to Pleiku and anyone carrying that much money was certainly a target, we were lucky. Jolys and I never established a set schedule and were only in an ambush once, and that day we were part of a large armored convoy. But still, my remaining time in B-24 had other exciting, challenging, and at times troubling experiences.

# OCTOBER–NOVEMBER 1969

## Polei Kleng

**A**s I settled into my routine, I began to see some of the insanity of military procedure. In mid-October, Lt. Light and I were sent to Polei Kleng to check birth and marriage certificates. The Vietnamese Special Forces were supposed to document who among the CIDG, our hired army, was entitled to family supplemental pay. Since every troop we hired claimed to be married and have four dependents, the maximum allowed, this raised a red flag with thousand piastres, so I would get fifty bundles. There was no possible way to count the bills, so I just counted the bundles. Then I put them in a mail sack, hefted it over my shoulder, and carried the fifty or so pounds of bills to the jeep. I know I must have looked somewhat like Santa Claus, but dressed in green and having no facial hair. Then Jolys and I drove back to Kontum, where I broke the bills down, still wrapped in bundles, and brought them to our camps over a two-day time period. The B-Team supported the following A-Camps, from north to south: Dak Pek, Dak Seang, Ben Het, Polei Kleng, and to the northeast, Plateau Gi, the only camp without any Americans.

We also had Mang Buk, north of Plateau Gi, which was turned over to the Vietnamese in December. Although I continued to pay at Plateau Gi, once Mang Buk was turned over, I was never required to visit and pay. I was never told why, and I never asked.

The camp executive officers, or their designee, usually the newest lieutenant on-site, would pay the troops, have them sign the sheet, and then return their excess funds and the payroll sheet to me. I would then add up all the monies that had been paid out, subtract that from what I had picked up, and, just like you do with your checking account, balance.

The only problem was that it didn't. After my first reconciliation, I had one thousand piastres left over, about one hundred dollars. That wasn't much, considering I picked up five million, but I remembered what the colonel told me after the $140 mishap at the club: "I expect you to balance." No "close enough for government work" for him.

I went through the entire payroll a second time and got the same results. I was very concerned, and then I thought, "You know, five million of anything is a lot. Since the bills were counted by hand, the counter might have made a mistake. If it is in my favor this time, maybe it will be in his favor the next."

So I decided to create my own "funds officer emergency fund." I had two safes: one an audit safe, subject to random audit, and a property safe, where I could store valuables for team members. The property safe was not subject to audit, and the auditor was not allowed to check it. I took the extra one thousand piastres and put them in the property safe. Now I balanced and reported that to Col. Hennigan.

"Good job, Lieutenant. I knew I could count on you."

Beaming, I saluted and left, wondering what my accounting professor would have thought of my solution. Based on my grades, I suspect he would not have been either surprised or proud. But I was pleasing the colonel, and that was more important.

Two weeks later I was audited.

Now I don't know how this would affect other people, but the fact that I was being audited did cause me some angst. I had to leave my office and wait until I was called back. The auditor was a first lieutenant, about my age, but obviously had done better in accounting than I did.

Finally he called me in.

"Lieutenant, what did you do?"

"I'm not sure I understand the question," I replied, my heart beating rapidly.

"You balanced. How did you do that?"

I may be an LSU grad, but I was smart enough to know that this question did not deserve a direct answer.

"Let me ask you this—is balancing good or bad?"

"Well, of course it's good, but no one balances."

"The colonel told me that this was simple addition and subtraction, just like a checking account. You draw money, you pay, and then what is left should be your ending balance."

"That's correct."

"So, since I balance, I did a good job?"

"That is correct. Congratulations."

But as he left, I could tell he was still wondering how I did it.

The next month I was five hundred piastres under, so I took that amount from the property safe, transferred it to the audit safe, and once again balanced.

Two weeks later, the same auditor showed up again for an unannounced audit and once again was amazed at my pristine books.

He went to the colonel, with me in tow, and announced to Col. Hennigan the following:

"Sir, I am not sure how this lieutenant is doing what he is doing, but he is by far the best funds officer I've seen, and I've seen them all. Would you mind if during his down time, we sent him around the country to teach other funds officers how to keep the books?"

Now Col. Hennigan was beaming as he said, "That shouldn't be a problem, but I don't want you working him too hard."

So it came to pass that on my twenty or so days when I had nothing to do, I would get on a helicopter and ride. And wherever it landed, I would ask the funds officer, "Do you have two safes?"

And then I'd reveal my secret, with an admonition that the secret had to be kept between us.

The colonel was happy, the other funds officers were happy, the auditors were happy, and my life was great. I was a hero, just because the colonel had made me figure out how to make sure I balanced. I guess he knew that a Louisiana boy could find an angle.

This may also have saved my life, because a typical lieutenant's assignment was six months of admin and then six months in the field, usually in reverse order, the field first. After six months as the funds officer, Col. Hennigan called me into his office.

"Lieutenant Bacque, you have been here six months, and I have orders assigning you to Dak Seang. I know you are anxious to go"—I really wasn't—"but you are too valuable to me and our mission. I can't afford to let you go, so I am sending Lieutenant Christianson in your place."

Two months later Dak Seang was hit by the NVA, and Lt. Christianson was seriously wounded.

And so it was that my entire tour of duty was spent in B-24 keeping the books balanced. And though I was subject to ambush on my many trips to Pleiku and anyone carrying that much money was certainly a target, we were lucky. Jolys and I never established a set schedule and were only in an ambush once, and that day we were part of a large armored convoy. But still, my remaining time in B-24 had other exciting, challenging, and at times troubling experiences.

# OCTOBER-NOVEMBER 1969

## Polei Kleng

**A**s I settled into my routine, I began to see some of the insanity of military procedure. In mid-October, Lt. Light and I were sent to Polei Kleng to check birth and marriage certificates. The Vietnamese Special Forces were supposed to document who among the CIDG, our hired army, was entitled to family supplemental pay. Since every troop we hired claimed to be married and have four dependents, the maximum allowed, this raised a red flag with headquarters, so we were required to go to all of our camps and make sure the required documentation was actually in the camp's possession. This was almost akin to vaccinating dogs that would soon be supper, as there was really no procedure for obtaining marriage or birth certificates in the hinterland where we worked. Most of the troops at Polei Kleng were Cambodians who'd migrated to the camp to make a living as soldiers. They had no organized religion, so they were married, as the Montagnards were, by the village chief, and their children were born in the village, so no documentation existed. But rules are rules, so Mel and I went to the camp to check.

There we found one marriage certificate and no birth certificates. We did find a general visiting, which caused a great deal of anxiety at the camp, since he was not expected, and supposedly he was there as the advance party for Gen. Abrams, the overall commander of MACV, Military Assistance Command Vietnam. Gen. Abrams had replaced Gen. Westmoreland, who had been recalled to the States.

The rumor turned out to be false, and after a few hours, the visitor departed. Since Mel and I could not do our work while everyone was entertaining the general, we were forced to spend the night and finish our investigations the next day, and since we were not expected to spend the night, naturally there was no place to sleep. As the most junior person, I got to sleep on a cot with no sheets, no blanket, and no pillow. I guess sleeping in the mud is worse, but I was getting used to the "good life," and this was far out of that sphere.

Because no documentation seemed to exist, we were forced to lower everyone's pay to the status of single. It was quite evident based on the number of women and children in the camp that many CIDG did have families, but "no papers, no pay" was the American philosophy. I actually was quite proud of myself, as I had found a great discrepancy and helped correct it. I had no concern that we were actually harming our allies: we had to do the right thing, even if it wasn't.

Once we finished our task and returned to Kontum, we reported what had transpired. To our surprise, Nha Trang headquarters had already been alerted by the LLDB (our Vietnamese Special Forces counterparts), and we were told not to pursue the discrepancies. We were to continue to pay, based on what was told to us, not what the records indicated.

That order certainly raised a red flag with me, and I wondered why the LLDB, who had very little regard for the CIDG and who really worked for us, were so concerned with our decision to pay based on paperwork. That question would be answered in a few months.

After returning to Kontum, I went to the MACV compound, located next door. There was a PX, as well as a shop that developed pictures, and I had some film to drop off. There I ran into a captain who had been part of the training cadre at Fort Bragg, who was assigned to CCC, Command and Control Central. That organization operated exclusively "cross border" in Laos and Cambodia. We were located in the tri-border area, so both countries were immediately west of our area of operations, and CCC was tasked with spying on, interdiction of, and prisoner snatches on the Ho Chi Minh trail. I thought that anyone choosing that duty had to be crazy, but this seemed to be a smart guy, and he was there. He shared a few war stories with me, making me even more leery of their mission, and then told me good-bye.

"Bacque, is that you?"

I looked behind me and saw a dirty ghost. I recognized him as a fellow OCS classmate, and from his patch I could see he was in the Fourth Infantry Division. But I could not remember his name, and he had no name tag on his shirt. He did look like hell, wearing a dirt-stained uniform, a day's growth of beard, and a weary look in his eyes.

I was dressed in pressed fatigues and shined boots, with my beret cocked over my eye.

"What are you doing?" I asked.

"I'm trying to get some new fatigues; we are out at Fourth ID firebase, just out of town, on stand-down."

There was a tailor shop attached to the PX, where we could get our uniforms tailored or rank and name tags attached.

"The tailor shop is next door," I said, "but you look like shit."

"I just got in from a thirty-day operation where we caught hell, and now we have a seven-day stand-down. I lost my blouse in the field and took this one off of a wounded guy. I'll be glad to get a shower and clean fatigues."

"Well, good luck to you." I shook his hand and left, feeling a little guilty. Here I was, sleeping in a bed with sheets, having a mama-san wash and press my outfits, clean my room, and shine my boots, *and* I was drawing jump pay, $110 per month extra, just because by the grace of God, I had ended up in Special Forces. Life was certainly not fair, but if someone had to be lucky, I was happy it was me.

In fact, I felt almost completely detached from the war. So far the only shooting I had experienced was artillery—ours going out and theirs coming in—but it posed no direct danger to me. For all the violence I had seen, I could still be in Fort Bragg. The only differences were that I was carrying a weapon everywhere I went and that I was riding in helicopters and jeeps rather than cars.

I have already described the CAPO officer, Lt. O, at Dak Pek, but the following incident once again had me call into question why the good die young and the reprobates seem to thrive. Lt. O had been in-country eleven months and had not taken an R and R. One day, when I was duty officer, he appeared at B-24 and announced that he was on his way to Hong Kong. He had not made arrangements, which was usually done several months in advance; he just decided to go. Since his job did not entail any expertise or responsibility and Jerry Alexander was his very able assistant, the colonel told him to go on. The problem was that he had to find a way to get there, since the roster of flights was full. Lt. O did not think this would be a problem and left for Saigon, literally thumbing his way. He carried over $1,000 of his own money and about the same amount from teammates who wanted him to buy things for them. Hong Kong was known for excellent prices, and he had his list. He asked me if he could get anything for me, and wisely I demurred.

Two weeks later—a week after he should have returned—he showed up. The colonel had not listed him as AWOL, knowing of his shortcomings. Since he would be going home in a month, no one was surprised by his tardy return. That day I was again serving as duty officer, so he had to report in to me. I was taken aback when I saw him. He was dressed in fatigues with no insignia and no brass. Instead of a beret, he was wearing just an army baseball cap. He was not carrying any luggage.

When he left he was wearing his summer-weight khakis, with all of his medals and brass, and was carrying a suitcase.

"What happened to you?" I inquired.

"It's a long story."

"I've got time. Tell me."

"Well, I had trouble getting a flight to Hong Kong; I had no reservations, so I ended up going to Taipei instead. The prices there were astronomical, so I was not able to buy anything on my list, except for two hundred LP albums; they were only twenty-five cents each. Now I need to buy some stereo equipment, so I can play the albums, but since I'm broke, I won't be able to do that for a while."

"That's only fifty dollars for the albums. What did you do with the rest of your money? And where is your beret and all your brass?"

"Well, I met a woman over there, and she ended up with everything I had, including my beret and brass. Luckily I had a round-trip ticket, so I could get back."

"What about the other money that the team members gave you?"

He looked sheepishly at me. "She got that too."

Several weeks later I visited Dak Pek and saw him again. He complained to me that he had a rash, which was really bothering him. Later he reported to the infirmary and found out that his lady friend had not only taken his money but also had given him an unwelcome present.

Lt. O wanted to stay in Vietnam, extend for six months, and make captain. His is the only situation that I am aware of that was refused. He could, and did, stay until his original obligation as an officer was up (two years), but he was not allowed to extend his duty for six months or be promoted to captain. I suspect Col. Hennigan had something to do with that.

On November 30, I celebrated my twenty-fifth birthday. Although I was still a second lieutenant, I would be promoted in ten days. I was older than most captains serving in B-24, due to my extended college tour.

Twenty-five: a quarter of a century. What, I wondered, lay ahead for me? I had been so lucky so far. Would it—could it—continue?

# THANKSGIVING 1969

Every holiday, there was a truce declared by both sides of the conflict. This meant that we would cease all military operations for the length of the truce, and "Charlie," the NVA and VC, could use that time to infiltrate more troops, build stronger defenses, and move large numbers of combatants without any fear of retaliation. Those decisions were made far above my pay grade, but I was always wondering why we kept letting this happen.

Since I had arrived in-country in September, Thanksgiving was the first truce I was able to witness. All of the camps were to be provided with Thanksgiving turkeys and trimmings, but only for the Americans at the camps, as this was not a Vietnamese holiday. The weekend before Thanksgiving, a large shipment of supplies, including frozen turkeys, was received in the B-Team, to be shipped to the A-Teams in the surrounding area. The turkey dinners were sent to the camps, but one of them, bound for Polei Kleng, was mishandled. By the time the mistake was recognized, it was certainly unfit to eat.

B-24 was the headquarters for northern II Corps and had six A-Teams attached to it. Of those six locations, Polei Kleng, located almost due west of Kontum, was by far the biggest problem camp—for several reasons. First, it was relatively close to Kontum, and there was a dirt road that allowed access between Kontum and the camp. This meant that keeping the indigenous troops on base was always a problem. The second issue was the ethnicity of the troops, who were largely Cambodians instead of Montagnards. Cambodians were not liked by the "yards"—the Vietnamese—and the feelings were reciprocal. Adding to the tensions at the camp, the Vietnamese Special Forces detachment was believed to be very corrupt and more interested in financial gain than in fighting the communists. This made for a volatile atmosphere and a great deal of ill will on both sides.

Now the camp had a spoiled turkey, and the Americans were wondering what to do with it.

This is the true story, related by Capt. George Dooley, the detachment commander, and excerpted from his book, *Battle for the Highlands*:

Five days before Thanksgiving, every detachment was sent a frozen turkey for the holiday. Our cook at Polei Kleng was an old Jarai woman who had never seen a frozen turkey before. When she received the bird, she put it under the kitchen counter and forgot about it. The day before Thanksgiving, one of the team members went looking for the turkey. The heat had both thawed and begun to rot the meat. It was a discolored shade of purple and did not look or smell very appetizing. Our medic, Andy Szeliga, said he doubted that it would be safe to eat, even though none of the team members had any desire to try it.

We called the B-Team and asked if we could get another turkey, even if we had to buy it, and if one was available, could they send it out by helicopter. Since we had the extra turkey, even though of questionable character, we decided to cook it anyway, and did so on Thanksgiving morning. Later that morning a fresh turkey arrived, and we cooked it as well, and ate it that afternoon. Now we were stuck with a rotten turkey, that after cooking, looked and smelled fine, so as gesture of friendship, we gave that turkey to our LLDB counterparts. The team consensus was that the worst thing that could occur would be for the LLBD to be poisoned and replaced by a new team, not such a bad outcome. The LLDB didn't get sick, so the situation turned out to be a win-win, all around.

A week after Thanksgiving, the C-Team commander visited Polei Kleng along with Col. Hennigan. After the obligatory briefing and reciprocating comments on the progress being made, Dai-uy Ha, the LLDB Detachment commander and I were walking out with the

C-Team commander when he asked: "Hey, what did you ever do with that poisoned turkey?"

LTC Hennigan, who knew what had happened with the turkey, mumbled: "It got taken care of" as he hustled the C-Team commander out the door. Dai-uy Ha just looked perplexed.

In the meantime, at B-24, as well as the other camps in the countryside, a meal of turkey, with all the trimmings, was enjoyed by all.

# DECEMBER 1969

By December, I was becoming comfortable with my duties as funds officer. Lt. Light had left in late November, so now I was on my own. The greatest benefit in his departure was that I inherited his bedroom. The officers were all assigned to a private room with a shared bathroom between two bedrooms. Lt. Light's room had a double bed, as well as a pink mosquito net. Where they came from, and why he had them, was not a conversation we ever had, but now they were mine.

December was also the month that Col. Hennigan instituted a new award, known as "The Boot." This was given to the officer who displayed the greatest incompetence or lack of military awareness. The boot award would remain in the possession of the recipient until someone did something to surpass the original faux pas.

The boot was a jungle boot mounted on a base and displayed prominently in the officers' club bar. Under the boot was a removable plaque, containing the name of the latest recipient. I was awarded the first boot, for something I thought was undeserving. In fact, before this incident, there was no boot award.

Early in the month, as I was taking my evening shower, an alert sounded. The fact that I was, even then, somewhat hard of hearing and that the shower blocked out the sound of the siren was not considered a valid excuse. When I walked out of my door, dressed for drinks, and saw everyone huddled in bunkers, I realized I might have a problem. That evening, in the club, the colonel approached me.

"Lieutenant Bacque, I understand that you do not think alerts apply to you."

"Sir, I'm not sure how to reply, but I do have what I consider to be a valid excuse."

"I am not interested in excuses. You are aware of our new award, are you not?"

"No, sir, I am not."

"Well, when you were seen nonchalantly walking to the club during a full alert, I made a command decision to institute a new award and allow you to be the first recipient. In a few days, you will see the manifestation of that award, but as of right now, you are the honoree. You have been chosen for ignoring the alert siren, and as part of the award ceremony, which we are having right now, you are required to buy a round of drinks."

"Yes, sir."

And I did.

I kept the boot for a short while until Maj. Ramos's pet dog left a doggie deposit on the colonel's rug. It seemed to me that Maj. Ramos and I were the most common recipients of the boot, but it was all in jest.

Maj. Ramos had replaced Maj. Billy and was much more "military" in his bearing and demeanor. He was also a "by the book" military man, which caused some friction with the junior officers in camp.

December was also the month when I became a first lieutenant, with an increase in pay of sixty dollars per month. On December 10, the day I was supposed to be promoted, Maj. Ramos and I went to Dak To to welcome an operation back from the field. Capt. Gray, who had gone to Dak Pek to take Capt. Kazanowski's position, was commanding a company from Dak Pek. They were participating with two other companies conducting a three-company sweep in the Tu Mrong valley. The Dak Pek element had made contact, the day before, with an NVA group of unknown size, and was getting artillery support from a Vietnamese artillery battery. One of the shells landed short, and the shrapnel killed Capt. Gray. After that occurrence, a decision was made to extract the troops. My friend, Jerry Alexander, was on the operation, and I wanted to meet him because I had more bad news. Our friend, Jack DaCosta, who had been forced to pay his own way to Vietnam, had been killed at Duc Lap, and I didn't want Jerry to hear it through the grapevine.

So Maj. Ramos and I were on the airstrip when the extraction helicopters started to land. I shared the bad news with Jerry and saw him get on a chopper to go back to Dak Pek. In the meantime, the CIDG soldiers, who had been on the operation and were paid at the airfield, were catching rides into Tan Canh, a small town just down the road, and buying supplies, including livestock, to take back to camp with them. As they returned, we put them on helicopters for the flight back to their respective camps. As I was loading one of the copters, a small pig jumped out of the arms of a CIDG and bolted for freedom. The CIDG, fearful that he would be left if he pursued the escapee, remained on the chopper, but I, seeing the severity of the problem, immediately gave chase. As I gained on the fleeing porker, with a kick I swept his legs from under him and quickly scooped him up and then returned him to the jubilant owner. Maj. Ramos, witnessing this act of selfless bravery on my part, vowed to recommend me for a valor award, with "P" device. No such award existed, so it was never awarded. That night, at the officers club gathering, Maj. Ramos reported my story as part of my promotion party. Col. Hennigan pinned my silver bar on my collar, explaining that I was not officially a first lieutenant because for some reason the orders promoting me had not arrived. But he added, "Screw the orders; it's your turn to buy."

I found out later that night that not only were my promotion orders screwed up, but also the duty clerk had made a mistake and I was scheduled for duty officer. Under the influence of way too much alcohol, I staggered to the TOC to begin my duty, hoping the local enemy would take pity and allow me to have a quiet night; they did. But that night I again witnessed the vagaries of war. The duty NCO was an E-5 working in the S-2 section. At about two o'clock in the morning, we began discussing the various weapons available to us. SF had many different armaments in B-24, and we could "play" with any of them that we wanted to. That afternoon we had been firing both a Swedish K and an Israeli Uzi during an impromptu target practice.

"Lieutenant, could I see your .45?" It was the sidearm I carried as the duty officer.

I handed it to him. Not believing what I was seeing, I saw him pull the slide back and chamber a round. All of my senses were signaling danger, but surely, I thought, this man knows what he is doing. After all, he is a Special Forces qualified soldier.

"Lieutenant, see the map of the bunkers on the wall?"

I nodded affirmatively, wondering where this conversation was going.

"My position is in that bunker right there."

He pointed the pistol and squeezed the trigger.

The TOC, where we were sitting, was made of concrete-block construction, buried in the ground and covered with several feet of dirt. It was built to withstand a direct hit from an NVA rocket. It was constructed in an octagonal shape, and the map was hung on one of the walls facing us. The reverberations from the shot, as well as the sound of the round hitting the wall, had me almost in shock. The TOC was filled with smoke but eerily silent.

As the shot rang out, the sergeant blanched a pasty shade of white, and his ears got beet red. I suspect that he was tired and had no idea what he was doing, and I was too stunned to say anything.

The bullet hit the map, right where he'd aimed and then began ricocheting around the room, finally lying spent against the wall behind us.

The sergeant looked at me with a ghastly look on his face, probably thinking he would surely go to jail for this. He meekly ejected the new round in the chamber and handed the weapon back to me.

"Lieutenant, am I in a world of hurt over this?"

"Sergeant, you scared the shit out of me, but it appears that other than the map having a hole in it, no harm was done. I'm willing to forget about this ever happening, but never let me catch you playing with a loaded weapon. I just thought you knew what you were doing; I am as much at fault as you. Now let's forget it."

Nothing was ever said about the incident, and no more accidents occurred.

On December 20, we launched Operation Gray, which was supposed to trap and destroy the enemy element Capt. Gray had been pursuing when he died. I was sent to Dak Pek, along with Capt. Rodriguez, to run the FOB (forward operations base) for the maneuver. In this case I was assigned to the S-3, the operations officer, to be his gofer. The operation itself went very smoothly, but no enemy was found. We had reports of groups moving through the night, carrying torches, the day before we launched. As was often the case, the enemy had been tipped off.

As Christmas approached, I was one of the lucky ones to be invited to a Christmas gathering with a family in Kontum. On the evening of the twenty-third, I went to the home of the chairman of the Kontum Province Council. Though I spoke no Vietnamese, it was assumed that I was somewhat fluent in French. I went to the home, spoke the little French that I did know, nodded when spoken to, and grunted when expected to reply. I'm sure they thought I was stupid, but I was able to eat with chopsticks, and that was some redemption.

On Christmas Eve, a visiting priest agreed to say midnight mass. The only problem was that he started drinking in the club with all of us at around 8:00 p.m., and by midnight we were all plastered. I read the epistle, and the father staggered around the altar. Mass was celebrated in fine form, and we retreated back to the club to finish my first Christmas in a foreign land.

# WHEN PIGS FLY

In late December 1969, between Christmas and New Year's, I was prepared for another routine trip to Dak Pek to deliver the January monthly payroll sheets and payroll funds for the CIDG troops. Routine meant that I would board a helicopter assigned to B-24, fly to the camp, drop off the funds to Lt. Jerry Alexander, and return. For those trips I carried a briefcase, filled with about one million Vietnamese piastres, about one hundred thousand American dollars at the official exchange rate. I carried a .45 caliber pistol, my M-16, and extra ammo for both, just in case. The trips were usually noneventful, and I had no reason to think that this one would be any different.

My flight was scheduled to leave in the early afternoon, so at the appointed time, I went to the helipad, where the chopper was waiting. I was supposed to be the only passenger, and as I approached the bird, there was no one, other than the crew, visible. As I reached the open doorway, I was shocked to see (and smell) five potbellied pigs, legs securely trussed, lying on the floor of the chopper. These were not the cute, miniature potbellies that were so popular many years ago, but large, smelly, and obviously unhappy animals that each weighed much more than I did. There were four females and one male, and they took up the entire cabin floor. I asked the pilot, who was standing beside me, "What's going on?"

"These pigs are riding with you to Dak Pek," he replied. "Something to do with improving the breeding stock. That's all I know. Get in; we need to go."

As I gingerly stepped around the pigs, trying to reach the seat that spanned the back of the cabin, they showed their displeasure by snorting and bleating. I seated myself in the middle of the cabin, secured my seatbelt, and placed my feet, having nowhere else to rest them, on the ribcage of the boar. He was lying on his side with his feet tied securely, or so it seemed. He glared at me with one eye, clearly displeased with me and his situation.

As the pilot started the engine and it came to full rotation, the pigs continued to show their displeasure with modern transportation by increasing their sound levels and trying to free themselves. As we started our takeoff, the cargo added defecation and urination to the snorts and bleats. Luckily we were flying with both doors open, so the smell was somewhat dissipated by the breeze.

I suspect that had we flown directly to Dak Pek, the rest of the flight might have been uneventful, but for some reason that I cannot recall, we landed in Dak To. Level flight seemed to calm the porkers, but landing and taking off made them very nervous and also raised my alert level.

As we approached Dak To, the amount of agitation increased dramatically, but when we landed, they seemed to settle down. Unfortunately, we were faced with another takeoff, and that sent them all into another frenzy of urination and defecation. Also, I noticed the boar, which was the most agitated as well as the largest, seemed to be getting free from his restraints. He was supposedly securely tied with all four feet wrapped in twine, but as he struggled, one of his front feet started to become loose. As he was situated right in front of me and I was the closest person he could take his frustrations out on if he got free, I became concerned. Then I decided that if I sat on his head, I could hinder his attempts to get loose, so that is what I did. I can tell you that I did not think this action through; I just reacted. The pig was not pleased by my move, and he proceeded to intensify the struggle. Out of the corner of my eye, I could see the crew chief laughing, as he was obviously describing the scene to the pilot. The aircraft commander turned in his seat, surveyed the scene, and then handed me a .38 and said, "Shoot him." I was in a quandary—all the hydraulic lines ran through the floor of the ship. What if the bullet went through the pig and severed a line? Besides, this must be a valuable pig, and executing him might endanger our relationships with the camp personnel. I was sure I could handle the situation; after all, I was a Green Beret. I waved him off and said I was OK. He shrugged and went back to piloting the craft. We were passing over Dak Seang, so I knew we were twenty to thirty minutes out of Dak Pek, and I felt that I could control the situation for that length of time.

Then it got worse. His second front leg worked free. The pig now was attempting to get up, and I was still on his head. Luckily for me, the floor of the helicopter was aluminum and very slippery, especially with the additional deposits made by the pigs, so the boar was having a very difficult time trying to rise. He was, however, bucking in such a way that we were inching toward the open doorway. At that moment I started thinking through what I had done and the very possible repercussions. If the pig got to the door, there was a very real chance that it could throw us both out of the chopper. Even though there was no doubt in my mind that this was a Vietcong pig, I suspected that I would get no medals for perishing because of his actions. Also, how would they describe my death to Cookie and my family? All these thoughts raced through my mind in an instant. As the pig continued to inch toward the doorway and the crew chief stared in awe, I reached out and grabbed the center post that supported the roof and held on for dear life. Now I had some leverage to apply to the pig's head and keep it on the floor, but how long could I hold on? I hoped the pilot would not dawdle on the rest of the flight.

After what seemed an eternity, I felt the rotor pitch change and knew we were preparing to land at Dak Pek. Once again the cargo voiced and expelled their displeasure with the flight as I held on for dear life. As the chopper touched down and I relaxed my hold, the boar leaped out of the chopper and fled down the runway, rear legs still tied, probably never to be seen again. I managed to reach my briefcase and M-16 without soiling my uniform too badly and turned to greet Lt. Alexander, who was highly amused.

"Thanks for bringing my pigs out; hope you all had a pleasant flight."

I don't recall my retort, but I handed him the briefcase and had him sign for it without counting the contents. He could surely sense that I was not happy. I was getting back in the copter when the pilot, a warrant officer, turned to me and asked, "Who is going to clean my chopper?"

Since I, a lowly first lieutenant, was the highest-ranking person in the group, I quickly answered, "Not me—get your crew chief to do it."

The floor of the chopper was indescribable, covered with the evidence the pigs had left behind. I was told to remain on the helipad, and I did so. The pilot, obviously a very astute person, took off and landed a few hundred yards away, in the middle of the swiftly flowing Dak Poko River. The water was about three inches above the floor, and in just a few minutes, it had washed out the chopper. During this maneuver, I remained on the ground, observing. When the chopper was clean, the pilot returned and picked me up, and we headed home, all with an amusing story to tell. As it turned out, this was my closest brush with death during my tour: almost killed by a VC pig. As a postscript, I found out from Lt. Alexander that the renegade pig was captured after I departed and placed in a beautiful new pigsty that he had built for the group. Several months later, as they were doing what pigs do, a 122 mm rocket made a direct hit on their sty, and they left this world. I suspect the VC or NVA had no idea they had killed one of their own.

As was the custom, we had a Christmas truce that lasted until New Year's, giving the NVA and VC time to rearm, reinforce, and rebuild their armies. They must have thought we were the stupidest people to ever fight a war.

We ended the decade on New Year's Eve with the most raucous party I have ever attended. It started at 9:00 p.m. at the officers club, but for some reason that bar was closed at 11:00 p.m., and we all moved to the enlisted club. Col. Hennigan appointed himself as the bartender and tended bar until 3:00 a.m.

In my letter to Cookie, I wrote:

I have never seen so many people so drunk in my life. At midnight everyone started kissing everyone else, and there were just guys in the club. It really looked like a gay bar; if an uninitiated person had walked in, he would have wondered what in the hell was going on.

The truth was that we were special soldiers, and we knew it. But pictures were not allowed, and no one mentioned anything about what went on the next day. I suspect very few remembered.

# JANUARY 1970

On New Year's Day, I woke up with a terrible hangover but looked forward to a Filipino pig roast, which would be prepared by some of our support staff. I had been a participant in many Puerto Rican–style pig roasts; my dad had mastered that art shortly after he and Mom had married, and I was wondering how the Filipino version might differ. It didn't. The fact that this was a new decade, the end of the sixties, was completely lost on me. It, except for the pig roast, was just another day at war—well, my version of war.

During January it was almost as if the war, for us, stopped completely. There were a few troubling incidents, but not war-related. Col. Hennigan was "asked" to come to Nha Trang and become a staff officer, allowing Col. Healy, the commander of Special Forces in Vietnam, to appoint one of "his team" to command B-24.

Col. Healy seemed to hold himself in very high regard and liked to be referred to as "Iron Mike." The troops nicknamed him "blind Mike" for the thick glasses that he wore, but never to his face. How he treated Col. Hennigan has certainly tainted my feelings toward him.

Col. Hennigan was a disciple of Col. Rheault and was not a favorite of Col. Healy.

Col. Rheault had commanded Fifth Group when the CIA executed a Vietnamese double agent about six months before. Col. Rheault was told of the incident but decided to remain quiet to protect his troops, and when Gen. Abrams asked him about the incident, he lied. Gen. Abrams knew the answer before he asked the question, so in a way, he trapped Col. Rheault. Abrams was not a fan of Special Forces, and he was not a fan of ours. Col. Rheault was arrested, placed in the Long Binh jail, and held for trial. When the CIA operatives refused to testify because of national security restrictions, charges were dropped, and Col. Rheault was shipped home. He at first was replaced by Col. Lemberes, a "Leg" (non-Airborne) tanker disciple of Gen. Abrams. The command sergeant major convinced Col. Lemberes that he needed to be Airborne qualified, even if he was not a real Green Beret, and took him up in a plane to make his qualifying jumps. After the third jump, Col. Lemberes broke his leg, and Gen. Abrams decided that maybe Special Forces should be commanded by a real Green Beret, so Col. Healy was chosen. There were, according to the rumors I heard, hard feelings between the disciples of Col. Healy and the disciples of Col. Rheault. Col. Hennigan had been on Col. Rheault's staff, and so in Col. Healy's mind, he was tarred by that association. With that as the backdrop, he transferred Col. Hennigan to Nha Trang, but not for long.

Col. Hennigan had friends in high places, and he vowed to fight the transfer. In the end Col. Hennigan won that battle, but it may have cost him the war, as he never got promoted beyond lieutenant colonel. Of all the officers I was associated with, he was the one—not only in my opinion but in all who served with him—most deserving of promotion. But after Vietnam, his career was finished.

And the bad news continued.

I heard that my counterpart in B-23, located in Ban Me Thuot, "lost" 120,000 piastres, the equivalent of $12,000. No one was saying what happened, but he was in deep trouble. Col. Hennigan made a point of relating the story to me directly, with a clear admonition that something similar better not happen on his watch; I became even more careful.

As he became more comfortable with me, Col. Hennigan continued to give me more responsibility. He assigned me to be his liaison to the Twenty-Fourth Sector Tactical Zone, which had responsibility for the entirety of Kontum Province. I was to attend the daily briefings and report back to the colonel. I suspect he found the briefings both boring and a waste of his time, so why not send me in his place? I assumed it was not a huge affront to send a first lieutenant to sit in for the colonel, and I just did what he asked me to do. Anyway, I found it interesting.

Later in the month, I was awarded my second "boot" award for going to Dak Pek with the keys to the S-1 jeep. It was reported, obviously incorrectly, that I had taken the jeep to Dak Pek. I was told that if I received the award for the third time, I would have my name inscribed permanently on the plaque.

That week, I was sure I'd earned the third award, as I was locked into the S-1 building by Capt. Galloway, the S-1. I was working late, and he did not notice my light on. He said that he called out, and hearing no answer, he locked the door from the outside and left. Due to my impaired hearing, I was unaware that this had transpired until I attempted to leave. Since I had no key, I was forced to call the TOC and get the duty officer to free me. That was not the most embarrassing part, though. While I was being freed, the duty officer pointed out that the door was a Dutch door design and the bottom part was not locked. I could have just pulled it open and gotten out through the bottom. Although I escaped the "boot" for that escapade, it was probably due to the fact that I was working very late.

Cookie and I started discussing R and R, which we were planning for June. Cookie was teaching school, and June would work for her. I thought June would be great because by then I would have been in-country for nine months, and after R and R, my time in-country should really fly by. Cookie had joined a "waiting wives" club in Lake Charles. Several friends of hers were in it, and they gave each other moral support. One of those was Jeanne Fehrenbach, whose husband was flying planes out of Cam Ranh Bay and had come to Vietnam about the same time as me. Cookie wanted Jeanne and Tex to take R and R at the same time we did, so we would have someone to "play with." I was only interested in playing with Cookie, but I told her that I had no problem with us meeting up in Hawaii.

R and R was something we all looked forward to. Each soldier was able to take an R and R to Hawaii, Hong Kong, Taipei, Bangkok, or Australia. The married men mostly chose Hawaii, with single guys heading to Australia or Bangkok. Our preference for getting the date we desired rose in relation to our time in-country. We became eligible after six months, but the priority continued to grow with each additional day we waited. By waiting until June, I was pretty sure I could get any date I wanted.

One of the captains, the detachment commander at Dak Seang, approached me about that time regarding his R and R plans. I would often help out in the S-1 shop when I had free time, and this was one of those times.

"Lieutenant Bacqué, I need to go on R and R the first week in March; can you arrange that?"

"Captain, the way it works is you request a date and see if it is available. There are no guarantees."

"I understand, but you need to make this happen. My wife and I are trying to have a child, and she will be fertile at that time. You need to let them know that."

I was somewhat taken aback, as this was more information than I wanted to hear, plus I had no control over the actual timing of the trip. But I assured him I would do all I could do.

He ended up getting his date, but whether he accomplished his mission was not something he ever revealed.

At this time, I wrote to Cookie about the beauty of Vietnam.

You know, Cookie, in all my travels around here, I'm really amazed at how untouched this country is by the war. You know that pictures of World War II show nothing but empty shells where cities once stood. Here it is entirely different. I'm taking pictures of the town of Kontum and the buildings in it. Kontum is really growing, with new buildings going up everywhere. This means the people seem to have confidence, so I guess we really are winning the war. The only traces of war that I see are the bomb craters and shell holes in the country. We can see them clearly from the helicopters, but even those are filled with water and look like round swimming pools. They are even aqua in color. Somehow you get very detached from war over here because of the peacefulness of the countryside and people. I guess if I were out in the middle of the fighting, I might have a different attitude, but I really find it hard to believe a war is going on. I tell you, Cook, this is really a beautiful country. I think, if it's possible, maybe in later years, I'd like to visit here and show it to you.

Thirty-seven years later, I was able to do just that.

And so January ended; I was one month closer to R and R and DEROS (date eligible for return from overseas), the day I would bade Vietnam good-bye.

# FEBRUARY 1970

As we moved into February, everything remained quiet, but Tet, the Vietnamese New Year, would occur on the fifth, and that caused us all to be a little nervous. The entire countryside was on yellow alert, the precursor to our modern alert system, and all American troops were confined to base. That did not affect me, as I was still expected to go to Pleiku and deliver my fund reports. Army life had no real days off; every day was just like the one before it. For Christmas and New Year's, we had some time off to celebrate, but mostly every day was like Groundhog Day. The only real recreation we had was a daily game of volleyball played against our CIDG guard detachment. The CIDG were all Montagnards, the tallest being about five feet high. If you looked at the American team, I was the shortest at five foot six. When we played against the CIDG, it looked like giants against midgets. If I were a betting man, I would have bet on us and lost my shirt. I don't think we ever won a game against them, and some scores were truly humbling. I suspect the only close games were when they decided to let us keep it close.

The weather in the highlands was actually chilly, with nighttime lows sometimes dipping into the fifties. That doesn't sound cold, but when you have become acclimated to one hundred degrees and 100 percent humidity, those nights felt cold. More than once I put on my field jacket, an item I was happy I had packed.

Different movies that had been sent to us were shown almost every night in a covered patio area. The quality of the movies varied greatly, and some of them outright sucked. The day before Tet, just such a movie was being shown. It was so bad I got up and went to bed. One of the troops, one of our guys, was so upset at the poor choice of entertainment that he threw a tear-gas grenade in the patio. No one knew where the gas was coming from, and because it was the day before Tet, panic ensued. Since I was in my room, Dave Cook came running in, yelling, "Gas!" Aroused from a deep sleep, I fumbled for my mask as Dave, obviously under the influence of alcohol as well as fear, stumbled into my beautiful mosquito net and tore it down. We managed to leave the room and find our bunker, but we were the only two who had donned masks. By that time the truth had been uncovered (although the culprit was not), and the all clear sounded. I was happy that it was a mistake, but getting back to sleep after that incident was not an easy task, especially after spending almost an hour trying to fix my mosquito net.

The next day was the eve of Tet, and that night the LLDB, our Vietnamese Special Forces counterparts, had a party in their officers club. I was working late, trying to get my reports finished, when several of them came in and got me, taking me back with them. Every other American officer was in attendance, and they wanted me to be there too. Since I was a late arrival, they suggested that I "catch up" by drinking three glasses of Vietnamese rum and two shots of strawberry wine. To refuse would have been an affront, so I did as asked. Then they gave me a Vietnamese Gauloises cigarette and told me to smoke it. I was very woozy and reluctant to make my condition worse, but all the Americans were egging me on, so I did smoke a few puffs on the cigarette, which I thought was vile. They laughed and said it was marijuana, and although at that time I had no experience with the weed, I was doubtful. I did feel like hell, and the cigarette did nothing to settle my stomach. I knew that if I puked in their presence, I would suffer a great loss of face and, by association, so would every other American in attendance, so I kept my dinner down by the hardest effort. Finally we were allowed to leave, and I was able to puke in peace, a terrible way to greet their New Year.

The next day, Tet, I decided to go to Pleiku and turn in my final reports for January. During this time, helicopters were hard to reserve, so my trip was in the S-1 jeep, with Jolys at my side. My friend Jon Wallace, who had taken over as S-1, asked if he could go, and I said sure. Jon and I had gone through OCS, Airborne, and Special Forces schools together, though he arrived in-country later than me because he went to language school. I decided another guard might be smart, and we had OCS classmates who were in the Fourth Infantry Division with a base camp just outside of Pleiku, so we jumped in the jeep and drove the thirty miles or so to Pleiku.

The roads were packed with traffic, as most Vietnamese wanted to be in their hometowns for Tet, and for many, that meant travel. I was hoping to be able to take pictures of the celebrations, but though I could go to Pleiku, I could not go into downtown Kontum. How could that make sense? But again, orders are orders. We made the trip there and back with no difficulty and actually visited some of our OCS classmates at Camp Enari, the Fourth Infantry Division's base camp. Because of our detour, the trip took up the whole day, but we were not concerned, as I was free to come and go as I saw fit. I forgot about Jon, though he didn't seem to be worried.

Jon was in the ordinary chain of command, and Maj. Ramos, who had flown out to Dak Pek that morning, had come back looking for him. He was told that Jon went off base with me during a yellow alert, when everyone but me was supposedly confined to base. When we returned, Jon was severely reprimanded. What could he say, that I had given him permission? Maj. Ramos knew that he could not actually reprimand me but he sure could make my life miserable, and for some time he did. We were able to avenge this tribulation by naming our pet python, Ricky, in his honor, but that came later. For now Jon and I had to absorb the punishment quietly.

Then an opportunity for revenge occurred. Maj. Ramos had given himself the position of boot-award chair and as such considered that he was ineligible to receive the award. Randy Stroud, another lieutenant friend of mine, and I decided to start sabotaging the major. We wrote anonymous letters to Col. Hennigan directly, laying out the major's transgressions, as well as beginning a series of practical jokes. The major was preparing for R and R and had started a serious diet. In the mess hall, each menu item had the number of calories beside it (part of an army initiative to stay healthy until you die). Randy and I started changing the calorie counts. The major was restricting himself to one thousand calories per day, and by the time we finished changing the menu, all he could consume was two glasses of sweetened iced tea and a toothpick. It took a week for him to catch on to our ruse, and he was plenty mad. But he seemed to get the message.

Midmonth Col. Hennigan and I were called to Nha Trang for a meeting requested by Col. Healy. He had every B-Team commander and every one of their funds officers in attendance to impress on them the seriousness of the job. I suspect the disappearance of the monies from Ban Me Thuot had a lot to do with this. He told us that we, the funds officers, were the most important people in Special Forces because we had the responsibility of handling a huge amount of money with very little control in place.

"Men, I want you to know how serious I am about your jobs. If I ever hear a hint of impropriety about anything you do, I will throw the book at you. That could include a court martial. As part of a new procedure, I have decided that every funds officer has to turn over his job four months before he leaves country, as that will allow us enough time to catch any problems before you are out of our reach.

"But I do understand that one of you has been doing a superb job, even traveling to other locations to teach best practices. I commend you, Lieutenant Bacque, as well as your commander, but I want you all to know that this is very serious business, and I will allow no screwups in my command. Is that understood?"

"Yes, sir!" we all shouted out.

"Dismissed."

We rose, and as we started out, I received congratulations from the other officers in attendance. The one that mattered most, though, was Col. Hennigan, and he was beaming.

But what would I do in my last four months?

"Don't worry, Lieutenant." Col. Hennigan said, "if you have to give up your job, I want you to be the new assistant S-3," which was a dream job. But I still had seven months left, so nothing was pressing (at one point the order must have been rescinded, since I ended up serving as funds officer until I left the country).

When I got back to Kontum, Jolys had a gift for me. He had asked me to get him a Polaroid camera, which Cookie was able to purchase and send to me. In appreciation he made me an honorary member of his tribe, the Sedang tribe, and gave me an engraved, brass Montagnard bracelet. I was appreciative because it came from him and had not been purchased in the market. Also, Cookie and I began planning our trip to Hawaii, which we were still hoping would happen in early June.

Things were going great; the war seemed to have been suspended, at least for February. In fact, in my letter to Cookie, sent at the end of the month, I commented the following:

> The newness of being over here has worn off, so there is really nothing exciting going on. Tet this year, as you know, was very quiet, with almost no enemy activity. It seems as if the war is over; maybe soon it will be.

It would not be long before I realized how wrong I was.

# MARCH 1970

The month started with a decision to "resettle" approximately twelve hundred Montagnards from their isolated villages to Kontum. Supposedly this was to give these villagers protection from the VC and NVA who roamed the countryside at will. No one asked the tribal people if they wanted or needed protection; it was decided for them. So, on the first of March, a fleet of helicopters descended on the villages and transported the occupants to Kontum. They left fertile fields, hunting grounds teeming with game, and comfortable houses. In return they were sent to a dusty field with battalion tents—an area more indicative of a ghetto than the open environment they were familiar with. Close to ten villages were resettled, and probably thousands of new enemy members were created. The misery of the people was evident in their eyes and expressions. There was no joy in Mudville created that day.

I was asked to accompany a medic from B-24 to determine what medicines they might need and what supplies we could provide. As we drove up to the refugee village, a pall of dust hung over the field. The villagers were lying about under the humid shade of the tents set up for their living quarters. In a typical village, the women would farm as the men hunted. They would rest in the shade of elevated structures made of bamboo, allowing the cooling breezes to circulate. The tents actually impeded the airflow, causing a stifling atmosphere. The only benefit was that the encampment was located beside the Dak Bla River that flowed through Kontum, so there was water for bathing and for cooling off if they got too hot. There was a beautiful sandbar adjacent to the bank, covered with women and children trying to find relief.

Two French doctors as well as several nurses were there to administer to the flock. And since I spoke rudimentary French, I tried to find out what we might supply.

"Why do you think this was done to these people?" a lady doctor asked me. After hearing my attempt at French conversation, she spoke in English.

"This is really for their protection. We could not offer them safe conditions where they were, and we can here." I knew that my answer was lame, but that was what I was told to say.

She rolled her eyes and turned away, going back to her task of healing the sick. What no one bargained for was the amount of disease that the cramped quarters and unhygienic conditions caused the refugees. There was no real plan, other than to move them. Once they were moved, we had accomplished our goal and could give ourselves a gold star. And once again, our superior attitude did much to turn the populace away from the government and toward the insurgents.

Over time, little by little, the people made their way back to the lands they had been taken from, and the tent city was shut down. But I wonder at how much we hurt our cause and enhanced the enemy's with this shortsighted decision.

Now that we had discovered the cooling waters of the Dak Bla River, we started leaving the compound every afternoon for a little dip. Capt. Strickler, the S-1 (admin), was curious about our absence and confronted us one afternoon. The "us" was Lt. John Ricci, the intel officer, Lt. Randy Stroud, the supply officer, and me.

What the hell are the three of you doing every afternoon; he asked. I suspect you are screwing off again.

We chose not to answer.

The three of us, the only lieutenants at B-24, had formed a group known as the Junior Officers Council. We would gather at least nightly and discuss the pomposity of the senior officers, except for Col. Hennigan, who was truly loved by all, and plot retribution. The most common target of our ire continued to be Maj. Ramos.

One night, as we were in Randy Stroud's room, in the midst of consuming four bottles of wine, Maj. Ramos came through the door in his pajamas demanding that we quiet down and go to bed, as we were disturbing his rest.

"OK, guys, it is past midnight, and all of us have work to do tomorrow. This party needs to be shut down right now." With that he turned and left.

"Were those pj's he had on?" asked Randy.

"Looked like it to me," John replied.

"They were baby blue, weren't they?" I added.

"I never thought I would see that in Special Forces," Randy added. "Well, it is late—let's take his advice and call it a night."

"Pj's."

And we all broke up laughing.

A bit of good news was announced around that time. We were informed that because of "Vietnamization"—turning the war effort over to the Vietnamese—B-24 would be shutting down by year-end, and almost all of our Special Forces troops would be going home. This was no relief for me, as I was scheduled to leave in September anyway, but we did have to decide what to do with the approximately $20,000 we currently had in our club funds. We certainly didn't want to turn that over to our counterparts, so a decision was made and the word was promulgated that the club account would be used to buy every B-24 member a Rolex watch. We were limited to the stainless steel model, which cost about $150 in those days, but when we left for R and R, we would be given the funds to purchase a watch. I suspect it was coincidence that Maj. Ramos and Col. Hennigan were both scheduled for R and R during March, but they were, and they were given their share of the club profits to use on their trips. Whether they actually bought the watch or not was never discussed; the final decision rested with each of us. But there was a belief that you could not be a true member of Special Forces until you had a star sapphire ring, a Rolex watch, and a demo knife. The club fund supposedly was taking care of the watch.

That decision, though, was later rescinded.

On March 12, François Sully, the famous French journalist, visited B-24 on his way to Dak Pek to do a story on the camp. Dak Pek, for some reason, was a favorite of visiting journalists. But before going there he wanted to visit us, Second Field Force, and CCC, our cross-border operation. Randy Stroud and I were assigned to escort him around, and we got an opportunity to get to know a wonderful person. He was the epitome of the dashing correspondent. Dressed in faded jungle fatigues and scuffed boots with several Nikons hanging around his neck, François's craggy face had a perpetual smile. A Gauloises cigarette hung from his lips, and he smelled of tobacco, and yet for all of his fame and notoriety, he was one of the most pleasant people I have ever met. He made Randy and I feel that what we were doing was as important as what he did. Francoise had been in-country since hostilities started, had been on many combat operations, and was then reporting for *Newsweek* magazine. And although he did not admit to it, it was evident that he thought we were in a losing proposition.

# RADIO RELAY

Col. Hennigan asked me to accompany an operation that would be working west of Polei Kleng, to man a radio-relay site. The radios we used were "line of sight," and the transmissions could be blocked by mountainous terrain. The operation, carried out by the Kontum Mike Force (a battalion-size group that was used for quick reaction to enemy attacks), would be in a valley perpendicular to, and within a kilometer of, the Cambodian border and the Ho Chi Minh trail. Because of the valley, a radio-relay site was established on a mountaintop that had been a firebase for the Fourth Infantry Division. Abandoned several months before, the bunkers were still intact and in good shape. A company of CIDG was sent to secure the area and provide security, and I went along with a sergeant to man the radios. The operation was to last a week, and the evening before we went out, the sergeant and I went to the firing range to test our weapons and make sure everything worked. While we were doing that, François walked up and asked me where I was going. I told him, and he wished me luck. We shook hands and never saw each other again. I felt a personal loss when I read of his death in a helicopter crash a few months later.

The next morning we were airlifted to the firebase and set up camp. Since the security detail seemed to be very professional, after checking the positions, I just sat around waiting for the radio to squawk. For the first day, that only occurred at night, as the operation personnel set up their night defensive positions and relayed to me their preplanned fire missions in case they were attacked. The sergeant and I took turns at radio watch all night, but nothing happened.

The next morning the radio came to life, not with a message from the Mike Force, but one from Col. Hennigan.

"Bacque, you left with my money locked in your safe. I am leaving this afternoon for R and R and need that money. A chopper is on the way. Get your ass on it and back here. You better not crash, and you better be here before I leave."

"Yes, sir," I replied as I began to hear the sounds of an approaching bird.

"Sergeant, I need to go back to Kontum, but I should be back soon. Do you think you can handle the radio until I get back?"

"Lieutenant, I've had a lot more experience at this than you have; don't worry about me. Just take care of yourself."

So I boarded the chopper and flew back to Kontum.

Upon arriving, I unlocked my property safe and found the colonel's money. That's what the property safe was for—to store valuables that the men wanted safeguarded. They would give them to me in envelopes that I never opened, with their names on the outside, and they would remain locked up until asked for. Usually there was not the degree of urgency that Col. Hennigan expressed, but he was the only colonel around, and his wish was my command.

After handing over the envelope, I went to the S-3 shop (operations) to see when I could get another ride out to the relay site. Capt. Dooley was the S-3.

"Captain Dooley, when can I go back out?"

"Our assigned chopper is on the way now, bringing out some resupplies, and by the time it gets back, it will be too late to go today. I will send you out on the first run tomorrow."

That meant that I could take a shower and shave, something that was impossible to do on the site, as there was no excess water. It had only been a day, but I felt dirty. So I had time to clean up, go to the club, and visit with the other two members of the Junior Officers Council. Randy was a combat veteran, so he was not impressed with my adventure, but John, who like me had not heard a shot fired in anger in our direction, was all ears. He was the intel officer and was aware of the mission and the ultimate objective, neither of which he could share with us since we had no "need to know," but he was interested in the details.

"WIA became KIA en route. Over."

"I don't think that is possible; it was reported to be a slight wound. Over."

"I can tell you he is KIA. Out."

I wrestled with whether to make that report to his friends and decided it s better for them not to know yet.

"Mike Force, Radio Relay. Over."

"Mike Force. Over."

"No word on Red Dog yet. Over."

"Thanks for checking. Out."

The operation continued for several more days and then was pulled out d returned to Kontum, as were we. But the evening before we were to leave, ird dog flew over our location, low and slow.

"Radio Relay, Bird Dog. Over."

"Bird Dog, Radio Relay. Over."

"I have a gift for you from HQ; I am getting ready to make a drop. Over."

"Roger. Will retrieve. Out."

He dropped what looked like a long map case, which landed in the middle the perimeter. I retrieved and opened it; the contents were six beers, some- at chilled and shaken to the point they were on the verge of exploding. e put them aside to let them settle, and that night the sergeant and I split varm six-pack. The operation was over—one casualty on our side and an known number on the other. Because of our limited diet, I had lost eight unds while just lying around, and I had been part of my first real operation. vas still not, and would never be, a combat veteran, but I did receive a word praise from the Mike Force executive officer for the professional way that ad handled the radios. The fact that I kept the truth about Red Dog from m was not an issue. I was proud of what and how I had done my mission, small as it was.

"What was the firebase like? Could you see traffic on the tr:
hear trucks at night?"

I had been so tuned to the radio that I had not even consid
were close enough to observe those goings-on. I promised mysel
aware when I went back out.

The next morning I was on the first flight and arrived midn
had no cooking facilities, so the sergeant and I were eating a cor
C rations, LRRP, and CIDG rations. The LRRP and CIDG were
we just added water and Tabasco for a very tasty meal. The C
other hand, were left over from Korea and were spotty: some wer
were crap. I brought out a case of Cokes and a case of beer, eve
had no way to cool it. The sergeant began to believe I was OK.

The operation went on for several quiet days while we waite
action. But at night I could hear the trucks and occasionally see
distance. We were on the top of a three-thousand-foot hill and h
visibility to the west. The Mike Force was operating in the vall
but because of the underbrush and vegetation, we never did actua
Then finally they got into contact. During the brief firefight, th
tain with the call sign Red Dog, was shot in the leg with what se
slight wound. A medevac was called, and he was airlifted out. U
he went into shock and died en route to Pleiku. The operation h
to pack blood expanders in the supplies. Had they been availat
might have survived. As it was, because of this oversight, the shi
and a directive came down shortly thereafter that any operation w
expanders on hand was subject to nonjudicial punishment.

That night was hairy, as the Mike Force had no idea of the
tion, or location of the enemy force. They called in the preplan
sions, and I could sense the urgency in the transmission. They als
Red Dog. I told them I would radio Polei Kleng and inquire.

"Polei Kleng, this is radio relay. Over."

"Radio Relay, Polei Kleng. Over."

I gave the fire mission coordinates in code and then asked
"What is the status of the WIA? Over."

# ROGER HENDRICKS ARRIVES

In mid-March the fourth member of the Junior Officers Council, Lt. Roger Hendricks, arrived. Roger took Capt. Dave Cook's room, adjacent to mine, as Dave was assigned to Dak Seang. He was not sent as camp commander but as XO. I know he was disappointed, but he was a soldier and did what he was told to do. Roger took over as intel officer, and John Ricci became his assistant. John was not qualified for Airborne or Special Forces but Roger was, so Roger became the senior, even though he was junior. They ended up becoming close friends, as all of us did; who was senior didn't matter a bit. All that was important was getting along and going home alive and together.

One of the first items on Roger's agenda was to visit the camps and see for himself how they were laid out and defended. Since I was frequently visiting all of them, I volunteered to be his guide. Unfortunately, we picked a day that followed a marathon drinking bout at the club, and Roger had not yet become expert at handling his liquor. Adding to that issue, our pilot was one of the wildest fliers I had experienced. He decided to make the helicopter mimic a roller coaster and, in so doing, caused Roger much discomfort. I saw Roger lean out of the door several times. This was very dangerous for the door gunner, who was situated in a cubby just behind the cabin, as the airflow tended to take anything tossed into it back toward his location, and Roger was tossing. I suspect we would have heard plenty if the gunner was in the direct path, and since we didn't, I guess he was sympathetic to Roger's plight. We had a marathon visit, hitting Ben Het, Dak Seang, and Dak Pek, and then back to

Polei Kleng, before heading home. Mang Buk was scheduled to be turned over to the LLDB that month, so we saw no need to travel there. When we got back to the compound, we had dinner, and then Roger went straight to bed as I headed to the club. At 9:00 p.m., I decided I too was ready for sleep and retired, only to be awakened at midnight by Col. Hennigan wanting company for a sing-along. At 1:30 a.m. I was able to go back to bed; Roger never joined us. The colonel had just returned from R and R and was in a wonderful mood. It was amazing how a few days of marital bliss could change one's outlook on life. The colonel was also awarded the boot because he had not sent any postcards to us from Hawaii letting us know what was "up." He very good-naturedly accepted the award.

The rainy season was in full swing, and it rained almost every day. We knew that historically this was the time that "Charlie," our nickname for the enemy, would take advantage, since air support would be limited by the weather. Roger couldn't tell us anything, but he did look more worried than usual.

As March came to an end, we looked forward to Easter, which fell late in the month, and hoped for more quiet times. On that note we would be disappointed.

# LEPROSARIUM

Leprosy was still a problem in Southeast Asia, especially in Vietnam. The lepers were still ostracized and found care only in a leprosarium. Those who were from the Kontum area were lucky because a Catholic nun, Sister Martine, had built a beautiful facility in a park-like setting. She was expert in sourcing building materials as well as supplies from our troops and local businesspeople. The facility she constructed was an oasis. My letter to Cookie, describing my visit, said the following:

> It looks like a park, with everything neat and clean and a facility that you would not believe. There are horses to ride, as well as pet deer just wandering around. There is a pigsty, clean as a whistle, with pigs so big they must weigh several hundred pounds. There is a beautiful church that was built by the residents, as well as a school and a farm. In addition, while we were visiting, Sister Martine showed us how she was diverting the river that ran through the property so she could use the river bottom for more land. That diversion was being done by the schoolkids who had gone to Kontum to pick up the rocks necessary for the project. It truly is a "garden of Eden."

Randy and I had gone to distribute candy that Cookie had sent, and the children were so appreciative. As we left, Sister Martine thanked us and mentioned that she would see us soon on her next visit to B-24. We both wondered what she would be asking Col. Hennigan for this time.

# APRIL 1970 DAK SEANG

Because Easter was in late March, I did not go to Pleiku to pick up my funds until March 31. On that occasion I drove with Jolys; I stayed at the C-Team, and Jolys stayed in town. I was awakened early on April 1 by the duty officer, beating on my door.

"Get up, Bacque, Dak Seang has been hit, and it looks serious."

I had been up late the night before, playing poker, and was unused to being rousted from my bed so urgently. Usually a visit to the C-Team was a pleasant experience, somewhat like a vacation. The visiting officers' quarters were located around a beautiful swimming pool, the grounds were immaculately landscaped, the food was of gourmet quality, and all the visitors were treated with the greatest of hospitality. But this morning was different.

I pulled on my fatigues and went to the TOC, where I learned that Dak Seang had been attacked early that morning, a furious battle was still raging, and at least one of the American defenders had been wounded and was en route to the hospital just down the road. I jumped into the jeep and sped to the hospital, where I saw several stretchers with CIDG on them being wheeled into the facility. I told them I was from B-24 and was worried about the American I had heard was wounded. I was told that it was Lt. Christianson who took my place at Dak Seang so I could continue as funds officer. I was told he was already in surgery but that his injuries were not life threatening. I found out later that morning that when the attack started, he immediately went to the observation tower to try and direct counter battery fire. While he was in that position, a B-40 rocket hit the tower, and he was blown out of the tower and fell to the ground. His life was saved by a sandbag that absorbed most of the blast and shrapnel.

I returned to the C-Team, knowing that I had to return to B-24 as soon as possible. I went to the funds office, got the money, and found Jolys waiting for me with the jeep. We knew that the trip back might be dangerous because it was unclear if this was the beginning of an overall offensive or just an isolated attack. In any case, we went home at full speed with our weapons locked and loaded. On arriving at B-24, I was informed that Col. Hennigan was calling a staff meeting at 1:00 p.m., just after lunch.

On entering the briefing room, which was crowded with not only SF personnel but also representatives from Second Field Force, I found a seat next to Randy Stroud. The colonel entered, and we all rose in deference.

"At ease," he said. "First I want to hear from Lieutenant Hendricks"

Roger stood in front of a map of the Dak Seang area of operations.

"We have been receiving intelligence over the past few weeks that led us to believe that something was going to happen soon, but we thought either Ben Het or Dak Pek would be the target. Dak Seang was a complete shock to us."

He went on to describe the units he thought were involved. He thought there had to be an alternative objective because of Dak Seang's isolation, but he had no intelligence to indicate what or where that alternate objective was.

Then it was Capt. Dooley's turn. He was the S-3, the operations officer.

"I did an aerial survey this morning, and the camp defenders seem to be holding well, but they need reinforcements. The NVA have surrounded the compound and are digging trenches toward the wire. If they get close enough to launch a human-wave attack, the camp could fall. We have TAC air all day as well as Spooky and Basketball tonight, but the antiaircraft fire is as intense as I have ever witnessed. They should be able to hold, if we can get some help into the compound." (Spooky was a DC3 equipped with a Gatling gun, an amazing defensive weapon; Basketball was a flare ship that could make the night into day.)

Col. Hennigan then stood and said, "I have decided to airlift a company from Plateau Gi into Dak Seang this afternoon. I want Lieutenant Stroud and Lieutenant Bacque to go in with that company."

When I heard my name mentioned, I experienced an anal stricture so intense that I almost fell from my chair. After what I had heard about the NVA surrounding the camp and the intense amount of antiaircraft fire, I knew that if I went in with Randy, I was a dead man.

I raised my hand.

"Yes, Lieutenant Bacque."

"Sir, I know this must have slipped your mind, but I just picked up my funds, and I need to pay all of the other camps in the next few days. If I go in with Lieutenant Stroud, that would be impossible, unless someone took my place as funds officer."

"You are right; let me think this over," he said. "Dismissed."

As Randy and I walked back through the compound, he turned to me.

"Bacque, I can't believe you are letting me do this alone; you are a chickenshit."

"Randy, you and I both know that whoever goes in there will die. I told you that I made a conscious decision not to die in Vietnam, and I have a good excuse not to go. Besides, it is sheer lunacy to try and land a company on the airstrip and have them fight their way in. I'm sorry, but you will have to die without me."

Randy and I were good-enough friends that he forgave my cowardice and went to prepare for his impending doom.

An hour or so later, he came into my office with a smile on his face.

"The colonel must have realized that his idea was not workable and canceled the air assault. I will live to fight another day, but you are still a chickenshit. Let's go get a beer."

And so, my closest brush with death, other than with the pigs, was over, and my friend Randy had forgiven me. For us in B-24, after almost six months with no war at all, it finally had come to us.

The next day I had planned on delivering the funds to the camps (except for Dak Seang), but there were no helicopters available for "ash and trash" runs, since they were all supporting Dak Seang. It was several days before I could get a ride to the camps, and when I finally did go, my chopper kept getting diverted. Finally, as we proceeded to Dak Pek, the last camp on my route, we had to fly in close proximity to Dak Seang, as it was in the same valley, just farther south. As we flew by, I used binoculars to survey the situation. The camp itself was covered in smoke and dust, and the trenches being dug by the enemy toward the outer perimeter were apparent. I was very thankful that I was not there.

At Dak Pek I decided to spend the night, something I did quite often. In fact I left a toothbrush there just in case I made the decision with little preparation. Dak Pek was usually the last camp I delivered funds to, and until it was time to pick up the reports and excess funds, I usually had nothing to do, so that night I stayed. When I was in the camp, I was assigned to a room very close to Jerry Alexander's, where a .50 caliber machine gun hung in an open window covering the airfield and river crossing. It was not my duty station. I really didn't have one; it was just where I slept.

That night, Jerry, Lt. Don Andrews, Capt. Udo Walther, and I gathered in the team room to talk about what was happening at Dak Seang. Even though the camp was only about twenty miles south of Dak Pek, it was still an isolated position. We at B-24 knew more about what was occurring than the occupants of Dak Pek, and they wanted to know what I knew. Udo had been the camp commander at Dak Seang before he came to Dak Pek, and he started the conversation.

"Bacque, for the life of me, I can't understand how the NVA got so close with no one being the wiser. Paul (the camp commander) must not have been sending out regular patrols."

I shrugged my shoulders and replied, "I am not sure what was going on, but this is what I do know: The NVA were able to set up their heavy antiaircraft guns on the ridges overlooking the camp. It appears that they anticipated us having to airdrop supplies, and when that occurred, they could shoot down on the resupply planes. As you know these planes have armor protection on the bottom, but not on the top. The Air Force is catching Hell. We've lost three so far, and now all the drops are being made at night."

Jerry asked about the air assault that had occurred the day before and that they monitored on the camp radio.

"Udo," I replied, "you know the abandoned fire-support base on Nui Ek?" He nodded. "Well, that—being the only flat surface close to the camp—is where Second Field Force wanted to land an air assault, using the ARVN troops. Charlie figured that out and laid a trap. I think we lost at least five helicopters and an untold number of ARVN casualties in that operation." The ARVN was the Army of the Republic of South Vietnam.

"Nui Ek is where the Cambodes set up during an operation and sent in false position reports," Udo replied. "They were spotted by a bird dog, and since we were not supposed to have any troops in the area, we lit them up with artillery. That's the last time they tried that shit." The Cambodes are almost as sorry as the ARVN's. I wish we had just our yards (Montagnards).

"I remember that—I replied, you had to send the team sergeant to another camp after that because the survivors threatened to kill him."

"Well," Udo replied, "Colonel Hennigan wants me to go back with you tomorrow to Kontum and then take over for Paul at Dak Seang."

"From what I hear," I answered, "it really is winding down—still a serious situation, but the chance of losing the camp seems to be over."

"Bacque, you still don't have your CIB [Combat Infantry Badge]. Why don't you come with me and get it?"

"Sir, I don't want it that bad. All I want is to go home when my time is up; being a hero is not that important to me.

Udo seemed taken aback; "You are different," he said.

"By the way, when you are in Dak Seang, who will be taking your place here?" I asked.

"It's only for a week or so, until a new camp commander can be assigned at Dak Seang, and then I'll be back; Don and Jerry can handle things here without me."

"Is there any concern that Dak Pek might be next? What do you hear? You attend the intelligence briefings every morning?" asked Don quizically.

"No one has any idea what they are up to; it appears that Dak Seang was the only target, and the NVA got whipped badly. If I thought Dak Pek was on the list, I wouldn't be staying overnight."

"Come on, Bacque; you know it would be exciting to be caught out here and have to fight your way back to Kontum," Don responded with bravado.

"I would call that stupid, not exciting, and I don't know about you, but I am impressed with Charlie. He seems to have picked a battle that, even though he can't win, he can sure make us pay a price." I changed the subject. "Guys, we talked about this earlier, and you asked me whether I thought that there might be another alternative objective, maybe Dak Pek. I told you that we in B-24 do not think so, but what do you think?"

Udo and Don both replied in the negative, but Jerry wasn't so sure.

"I have a premonition," he said. "I just get a feeling when I'm out on operations. I think the yards are feeling it too. I think that Udo and Don are right, but I am still just a little bit worried."

Even though I knew that the camp was well positioned and very well defended, I slept that night with my M-16 next to me, and I woke several times to look out the window with the machine gun to make sure nothing was amiss.

The next day I left on the supply chopper with Udo. He flew with me to Kontum, met with Col. Hennigan, and that afternoon flew into Dak Seang.

It was decided, very early, by higher-ups, that Dak Seang would be the model to show that Vietnamization could and would work. The relief of Dak Seang would be accomplished solely with ARVN and CIDG troops, albeit with their American advisors. And so the relief effort had started right after the siege began.

That meant that Second Field Force was now making all decisions, which placed Col. Hennigan and all of the SF warriors under Second Field Force's command. They obviously did not know the battleground, the enemy, or the capabilities of their troops because the breaking of the siege took much longer, cost many more lives, and exposed the shortcomings of the ARVN soldiers in grim detail. I had a ringside seat, as I was sent by Col. Hennigan several days after leaving Dak Pek to accompany Command Sergeant Major Campbell to the FOB (forward operations base) that had been established at Ben Het. The two of us handled the SF troops; various Second Field Force officers who had overall command directed everything else.

At the FOB, we would monitor radio traffic from the Mike Force battalions that were part of the relief effort. Each B-Team had a Mike Force (Mobile Strike Force) battalion assigned to it. These Mike Force units would be used as a reaction force when situations like Dak Seang occurred. In this case, multiple Mike Forces were moving toward Dak Seang to break the siege. I believe that the Nha Trang Mike Force, as well as the unit from B-23, were both part of the relief effort. One of the Mike Force units had an Australian advisor whose call sign was Kangaroo. These units were on our radio net. In addition, we monitored the ARVN units working in the area, and these transmissions made me start to question the eventual outcome of the war.

All ARVN units had American advisors assigned, who went to the field with them. I remember a radio call from one of the units requesting a medevac. When it arrived, the ARVN soldiers broke from their positions and tried to climb on the chopper to flee the battlefield. They were beaten back by the crew, and the helicopter lifted off, but the ground troops were still in heavy contact.

I listened as the advisor told us, in a calm voice, that they were being pursued by a large enemy force and needed close air support as they withdrew. Then I heard him say, in a much more agitated voice, that the ARVN were shooting at him and the other advisor. It appeared that the ARVN hoped that the NVA would slow down their pursuit to capture the wounded Americans. The radio went silent, and we never found out what happened. But this act of cowardice by our allies certainly started a change of heart with me.

Dak Seang, because of its isolation, could only be resupplied by airdrop because the runway was unusable. As I previously mentioned, the NVA anticipated this and had laid a trap. Heavy antiaircraft weapons were placed on the high ridges overlooking Dak Seang and threw up a murderous gauntlet of fire on any resupply plane. On April 2, the first plane was shot down, and the crew was lost. The second plane was lost on April 4 and the final on April 6; we lost both those crews as well. But the plane that was lost on the sixth had a more personal consequence for me.

As I mentioned earlier, one of Cookie's good friends, and a member of her waiting wives' club, was married to an air force pilot from Lafayette, Tex Fehrenbach. I had never met Tex, but Cookie had asked me if Tex and Jeanne could join us on R and R. I planned on meeting him in June.

Tex was flying out of Cam Ranh Bay as copilot of a C-7 Caribou. His squadron, commanded by Lt. Col. Roger Larrive, another native of Lafayette, was tasked with the resupply of Dak Seang. Here I was, on the ground, Tex was flying resupply, and Roger was his CO, all of us from Lafayette, Louisiana. What an amazing coincidence, though none of us were aware of it at that time. On April 6, as Tex's plane was making a resupply run, it was struck by fire. I spoke later to a FAC pilot who was flying support, and he relayed this story to me.

"I saw the plane take fire, but the crew finished their run. They asked me to look at the wing to see if I thought they should land in Dak To. It appeared to me that the damage was not severe, but I cautioned them that it was difficult to be sure. They could have landed in Dak To, but better facilities were available in Pleiku, where the resupply was being flown out of, so they decided to go on to Pleiku. About twenty miles from Dak To, the wing came off, and all aboard perished."

I knew that the plane had crashed, but I had no idea who was aboard until about a week later when I got a letter from Cookie telling me that Tex had been on a plane that was lost over Dak Seang. I never wrote to Cookie about dangerous situations, so she did not know about the siege until Tex's death. But now the war, for her, had become much more personal, and in a way, it had for me as well.

In her letter to me, I could sense that she was distraught; she was upset about the loss of her good friend's husband, and she was also worried that it had happened where I was. She questioned me as to the value of the sacrifice we were being asked to make.

In my letter back to her, I tried to find meaning in a situation that had none.

I got your letter today telling me of Tex's death, and even though I did not know him, I feel a great personal loss as well as a great deal of sympathy for Jeanne. But at times like this, no amount of compassionate verbiage can begin to quell the grief she must feel. We lost some fine men at Dak Seang, not only on those three Caribous that were shot down, but also in numerous helicopters that were lost as well. It's very easy, over here, with dying occurring all around you, to remain isolated from it all, until you find out that it happened to someone you know or knew. I consider myself very lucky to only have lost two friends, Bob Bruce, who died his first week in-country, and Jack DaCosta, who came to Pleiku with me. Times like these make you aware of the truly transient nature of life, and make you pray for just one tomorrow.

You ask me to give you a reason and a purpose for our presence here, and truthfully, I can't. I know that I am here because I'm in the army and was ordered to come. Tex was over here because he was a professional and it was part of his job. We can't rationalize the death of any man, because any death is a great loss to someone. That is just as true for our enemy as it is for us—one of the great conundrums of war. And for those directly affected by the loss, it is the greatest tragedy that could ever occur. I can't explain the purpose of this war, because in reality, war has no purpose. How can you make sense of killing another human being, or losing a loved one? Tex was an angel of mercy, not a dealer of death. But I suspect that the fact that what he did enabled ten Americans and four hundred Montagnards to survive a vicious enemy attack will give little solace to Jeanne. I have no words that will begin to bring meaning to her great personal loss; I can only hope that this war is ended soon, and that the specter of this war doesn't again touch someone we know or care about.

These are selfish sentiments, because we know that the dying will continue, and someone will be touched by that loss, until we are all back home. I have conflicting sentiments regarding this war, and really don't want to share them now. But I do hope and pray that this struggle is soon resolved and that all the troops return home. Tell Jeanne that I hope she can find consolation in the fact that Tex was doing a very vital and necessary job; and his sacrifice helped save many lives. But to Jeanne, that probably is little solace, since the only life that mattered to her was that one that was lost.

It's taken me a long time to write this letter, and I've chosen my words very carefully, yet it doesn't convey a tenth of what I am feeling. I have been very cautious in my writings to you, because I didn't want you to worry about me, and yet you have been touched by this war in a way that I could not prevent. I will continue to share the daily goings-on with you, and reassure you that nothing I am involved with has any degree of real danger. There is no doubt in my mind that I will see you in Hawaii in June and in Lafayette in September.

Love You,

Donnie

As the siege entered the second week, it was apparent that the attack had failed and Dak Seang would remain an operational camp. Now the effort to rebuild, reinforce, and restock began in earnest. The new Dak Seang would be better and stronger, according to the Second Field Force commanders.

# DAK PEK

On April 10, Lt. Don Andrews, the XO of Dak Pek, came to Kontum for an overnight trip and was regaling us with stories. I was duty officer that night, and he was in the TOC with me. To emphasize one of his tales, he stood on my desk, towering over me. Unfortunately he forgot about the ceiling fans that ran constantly, keeping the air in the TOC somewhat tolerable. The blades were metal, and one made contact with Lt. Andrew's ear, cutting him severely. He was immediately sent to the dispensary, where his ear was repaired and a large, white bandage placed on it.

On April 11, I flew into Dak Pek to pick up the funds report from Jerry Alexander, so I could finish and turn in my report. Lt. Andrews was on the same chopper, returning to Dak Pek. We flew by Dak Seang and could still see smoke and ordnance explosions as we headed north up the valley toward Dak Pek. I can remember thinking how lucky I was that I had not been sent there as ordered by Nha Trang. I landed at Dak Pek as dusk was falling and retrieved the report from Jerry. Usually I would spend the night there, but tonight there was an Australian floor show in Kontum, a cut above the usual Filipino shows.

"Are you staying?" Jerry asked.

"Not tonight. I'm going back for a floor show."

"You would choose a floor show over our hospitality?"

"It's Australian."

"Lucky guy. I don't blame you."

"How are things at Dak Seang?" he inquired.

"I think it's almost over; Udo is getting them squared away. I suspect he will be back here soon."

"I hope so; we miss him."

With that I boarded the chopper and flew back to Kontum and the show.

Although I do not recall the show and I did not describe it in my letter to Cookie, I do remember being awakened in the early morning with news that Dak Pek had been attacked by a large enemy force and that the American Hill, where the SF advisors stayed, had been overrun by sappers. There was limited radio contact, and no one was sure what the real situation was. I had no idea whether my friend Jerry was alive or dead, and I wouldn't know for sure until the next day.

Miraculously, all of the SF team members were relatively unhurt in the attack, and they were able to kill all of the sappers and, over time, repulse the attack on the camp.

I could have been there: saved by a floor show.

Jerry recalls that incoming explosions awakened him, and he took a few minutes to put on his shoes and grab his weapon. As he reached the door to his bunker, a satchel charge went off and knocked him across the room. He lay there holding the plywood door in his hands, thankful that it had absorbed most of the blast.

Not knowing where the sapper who had thrown the charge might be, Jerry escaped through the opening that held the .50 caliber, the room I would have stayed in. As he emerged from the opening, he came face-to-face with another sapper, whose mission probably was to destroy the .50 caliber position. Jerry was carrying an M-79 grenade launcher armed with a buckshot round, but when he tried to fire, the weapon fell apart in his hands. Luckily the sapper, whose eyes, according to Jerry, were as large as saucers, was armed only with a machete and thought better of confronting Jerry. As he turned and ran away, Jerry emptied his .45, missing him with every shot.

Jerry's duty position was down in the 4.2 mortar pit, and he was supposed to fire illumination rounds, so that is what he did, but first he made sure that no more sappers seemed to be in his nearby vicinity. After firing the first flare, he saw numerous shadows still running around the American hill. Jerry had positioned a case of grenades in the mortar pit and now started to pitch them at the black shapes scurrying around the hill using an airburst, by holding the grenades for a count of three before throwing.

"I always had a pretty good arm, and I could throw those grenades pretty far," he told me. "The NVA had no idea where I was and where the projectiles were coming from. I must have killed a bunch because all of a sudden, I didn't see any more targets. As I looked around, I saw no other Americans, and I had the harrowing thought that I might be the only one left alive and wondered how much longer that could last. I continued to fire illumination and occasional HE (high explosives) when targets of opportunity presented themselves. I can remember how scared I was, but I knew that I had to fight as long as possible.

"I heard Spooky come in," he continued, "and start making runs on the airstrip. I found out later that Lieutenant Don Andrews had gotten it diverted from Dak Seang, and the ship arrived just as the NVA massed for a human-wave assault across the airfield. They were cut to pieces, and at least several hundred casualties were inflicted. Had Spooky not have arrived, we would certainly have been overrun.

"Finally I had a faulty round stick in the tube, and I was so exhausted that I could not get it out. By then dawn was breaking, and I could see some other team members in the eighty-one mortar pit, next to the team hut. I went to their position and found, to my amazement, that all the team members were alive and functioning. That was the second miracle of the night, the first being the arrival of Spooky at just the right time. It looked then like we could hold, and we did."

While Jerry and his teammates were fighting for their lives, at B-24 we were trying to react. Col Hennigan decided to send Maj. Ramos in to take command of the camp and then changed his mind, deciding that whomever he sent would have a very good chance of dying on insertion. Maj. Ramos was considered too valuable to die, so Capt. Strickler, the S-1, was sent in his place. I remember him coming to my office to tell me good-bye. I remember thinking that it would probably be the last time I saw him; it wasn't.

After Capt. Strickler was inserted, successfully establishing radio communications became our greatest priority. Dak Pek was almost sixty miles north of Kontum, and the radios that were still intact did not have that range. So a decision was made to send all of the junior officers, in rotation, to fly above the camp that first day as radio-relay sites in the backseat of FAC bird dogs. Our job was to relay messages between B-24 and the camp. The aircraft could stay on station for several hours. At the end of that time, we would relieve each other, fly back to Kontum to refuel, and get a few hours of rest, and then back to Dak Pek.

The sky was filled with aircraft of all types, supporting the defense of the camp. There were F-4 Phantom jets as well as propeller-driven fighters, all waiting their turn. This deadly ballet was directed by another FAC on station. But that was not our mission: we orbited at about five thousand feet, high enough to avoid gunfire but low enough to have a perfect view of the camp, through binoculars. I remember seeing Don Andrews moving around the perimeter, his white-bandaged ear standing out in stark relief to the red soil he walked on and the green uniform he wore.

After our two-hour stint was over, the pilots would take us on strafing runs of the NVA trenches, and we would fire an M-79 grenade launcher out of the open back window. I don't think I ever hit anything because it was so difficult to figure out when to shoot, but we had fun shooting at them, and I suspect they had a grand time shooting at us.

Finally a new shortwave radio was installed, and our services were no longer needed, but for that day, I finally felt like I was in a real war.

The heavy fighting continued for the rest of the week, and then the NVA began withdrawing back into Laos—another battle lost.

# APRIL 1970: B-24

While still recovering from the shock of the attack on Dak Seang on April 4, I got another big surprise: Bill Brooks showed up. The last time I saw Bill, before this visit, was at the replacement depot just after we arrived in Vietnam. Bill had chosen to go to Jungle School, in Panama, so he was not on the same set of Vietnam orders. I had heard that he was assigned to MACV, Military Assistance Command Vietnam, which was considered the worst possible assignment to get. Knowing that Bill was as resourceful a person as God created, there was no doubt in my mind that he would be OK, but I did not think I would see him during my tour.

I was out of the compound that morning, delivering the funds to Polei Kleng, and when I got back, I was told I had a visitor. As I walked into my office, I saw Brooks sitting in my chair. He was wearing a beret, so I knew he had finagled his way back into Special Forces. I was really glad to see him, and we spent the rest of the day catching up. He had come to determine what B-24 was doing currently, and what Randy Stroud, who was then the B-24 psychological officer, was planning for the future. He and Randy had finished their visit, and now he just wanted to visit with me.

Soon we got to his story, and it was interesting.

After we left to report to Nha Trang, Bill found out he was assigned to a MACV compound in southern I Corps, called Mo Duc. He flew into Quang Ngai and was picked up at the airfield for a forty-five-minute jeep ride to Mo Duc. The trip was uneventful until they were about two miles out, when the driver radioed the camp that they were entering "Snipers

Gap," which was given its name after a team member had been ambushed and killed the month before.

"Bacque," he said, "the driver floored the accelerator, and we took off as fast as the jeep would go. We must have been going at least sixty miles per hour on a rutted gravel road, sliding from one side to the other. When we reached the turn off to Mo Duc, the driver told me that if we had not showed up within five minutes of the radio call, a reaction force would have been sent out.

"As we drove up to the compound, I could see several bodies on the side of the road. My driver explained that they were VC, and the bodies were left beside the road to make it easier for their families to retrieve them.

"After I put away my gear, I was asked to go to the helicopter pad and help offload a helicopter. The chopper was transporting the bodies of ARVN troops killed in a battle, and we were supposed to take the bodies to a mortuary just outside the compound. As the new guy, that was my assignment. Without a doubt, I knew we were in a difficult place, and I needed to get myself out. I started plotting my strategy that very day."

He went on, "The team was commanded by a major, who was a complete ass, and he proceeded to make my life even more miserable than just being there. Every day we were sniped at, mortared, and then yelled at by the major.

"I slept in a bunker. My bunk consisted of a wooden frame sturdy enough to support the railroad ties on top. They were there for protection from a mortar round that might penetrate the sandbags on the exterior roof. A parachute shroud as well as a mosquito net covered that frame—to prevent unwanted animal or insect visitors. But despite that perimeter defense, one night a lizard fell on my head and scared the crap out of me. I was getting more and more convinced that if I didn't leave soon, I would end up like Bob Bruce (who had died in October). No one knew paperwork as well as me, and I launched a barrage of paper to our headquarters as well as the SF headquarters. Finally someone paid attention, and I was transferred, and now here I am."

"Well, you are a sight for sore eyes. Let's go to the bar and get drunk."

That night, for the first and last time in my Vietnam tour, I was ordered to stand guard duty at an observation point on the camp perimeter. Because of Dak Seang and the uncertainty of the scope of the enemy attack, we were on high "red alert," so the entire compound pulled guard duty. Brooks and I, with little regard for the consequences, started happy hour a little early. Since I reported only to Col. Hennigan and had no other direct superior, there was no one to tell me what I should not do, and the colonel was not in the bar. He had flown to Dak Seang that afternoon to see firsthand what the troops there were facing. Capt. Dooley had gone with him and would end up staying for a few days. When Col. Hennigan flew back, he huddled with his staff, minus me, to fine-tune the defensive strategy. What I did was juvenile and probably made me subject to potential court martial, but I was young, impetuous, and stupid, so I did not consider the consequences. Our drinking continued until midnight, when I was to assume my position on the wire and remain there until 6:00 a.m.

My guard position was in a concrete observation bunker that was cold and damp, which probably helped to keep me alert. Brooks, realizing that he was as much to blame for my condition but would suffer no military consequences if I were court-martialed, decided to accompany me. He volunteered to help me stay awake, but within the hour, he announced that he was too sleepy to stay and told me that since I would not need my bed for the rest of the night, he was going to see if he could grab some sleep in it.

I knew that if I closed my eyes, for even a second, an NVA sapper, who I imagined was sitting just outside the lighted perimeter, would just walk up and slit my throat. I can't begin to describe the way I felt as the minutes dragged by, but by the grace of God—and the sheer discomfort of the bunker—I was able to stay awake and alert until I was relieved at 6:00 a.m. At that time, I went to my room and kicked Bill out of my bed. I was able to grab a few hours of sleep and then went back on regular duty.

That morning Bill needed to get to Pleiku to visit the C-Team, and I, having nothing better to do, decided to accompany him. Because of the high-alert status, I took him in the S-1 jeep and pulled a trailer, filled with Montagnard guards, behind it. My interpreter/bodyguard, Jolys, drove the jeep, and I rode shotgun. We delivered Bill to the C-Team with no obvious ill effects, and Jolys and I returned to Kontum uneventfully, except for my huge hangover.

Although the battles for Dak Seang and Dak Pek continued in varying degrees of severity for the whole month, life at B-24 was remarkably normal. Yes, one of the paradoxes of "my war." Although I spent some time at Ben Het in the FOB, my letters home seemed to indicate that there was no war at all, and for me, most of the time that was the case. The troops still had to be paid and paperwork done, and junior officers, as was expected of them, continued to get into mischief.

One consequence of the battles was the large number of awards that was generated. Col. Hennigan was told that every defender at both camps was to receive at least a Silver Star, but the citations had to be written and submitted for approval. As soon as Capt. Strickler returned from Dak Pek, he left for R and R in Burma. He was single, quite an outdoorsman, and he went there to hike the jungles. Our Junior Officers Council found that amusing, since there was plenty of jungle hiking available much closer to B-24.

When he left, I was appointed as his "acting" replacement.

During the twenty or so days a month when I had nothing to do in B-24, Capt. Strickler would often ask me to help him with normal S-1 work, but soon I was detailed with just writing up award recommendations. He liked my writing skills, and since he had plenty of other work to do, he ended up giving the majority of the awards work to me. Between the sieges of the two camps, there were over seventy valor recommendations that had to be written, and now he was gone. So now I had his work in addition to writing up the valor awards. I worked on regular S-1 paperwork during the day and valor awards at night. For someone used to a very unstructured job demand, I was busting butt.

Then catastrophe struck. The water well went dry, and we had no water for six days. Rumor had it that the VC was responsible, but that was never proven. One of the great luxuries of B-24 was having flush toilets, but with no water, there was no flushing. Several anonymous dumpers went into others' bathrooms to use the toilets, so their personal rooms would not be smelled up. Those people remain anonymous to this day, but the Junior Officers Council members were prime suspects.

No water also meant no showers, and although the temperatures were not extremely hot, we still got dusty and smelly. The only relief was sneaking into the communal shower in the local MACV compound next door. This was frowned upon, but after four days I couldn't stand myself, so I went. The hardest part was shaving, as we had to get water from a water trailer and use that cold water for hygiene. Regular troops did this all the time, but we were spoiled and complained bitterly. Finally the well was fixed—water flowed, toilets flushed, and showers worked. Our misery was over.

The job as acting S-1 was a chore. Since I was only acting and had no idea exactly what the S-1 did, I could not answer many of Maj. Ramos's questions. He was a stickler for detail and would get really upset with me when I could not answer his queries. I wrote to Cookie:

> I don't know whether I'm coming or going. Maj. Ramos keeps asking me questions that only Capt. Strickler knows the answers to, and he gets upset with me because I can't answer him. It's really pretty funny because almost all I do is sit behind the desk with a glazed look on my face and wonder what's going to happen next.

At least I was adept in the art of award-writing and was working my way through that stack. But then we were informed that a Silver Star recommendation for Sgt. Gary Beikrich would be upgraded to a Medal of Honor, and a whole new award packet had to be done. It took me and the staff assigned to help me several days to compile all of the material needed. We must have done a good job because Gary was indeed awarded the MOH, a very well-deserved recognition.

All of the Junior Officers Council members were well versed in kidding and playing practical jokes on one another. Randy Stroud, the senior member of the group, had been trying to get to Sydney for R and R for three months and could never get an available seat. He swore that I was sabotaging him, but that was not true. We knew we had to get him out soon because he was becoming very testy. Maybe it was because we called him the "White Whale" based on his complexion and size, but the final straw for him came one day when he was monitoring the radio. The most important requirement for monitoring the radio is to write down all conversations, so there would be a historical log to refer back to. On that day Ghost Rider 31, a chopper assigned to us, called in. Randy recorded it as "Ghost Ridder," and that triggered a response from the rest of the club. We started giving him books every day, ostensibly to improve his intelligence level as well as spelling skills. He received, over the next several days (anonymously of course), *Spelling for Beginners*, *The Idiot*, and *The Easy-to-Read New Testament*. We finally backed off after we noticed that Randy was eating even larger servings than before and really putting on weight. But finally, his R and R was approved for May 1, and now he needed to lose weight, so the Aussie ladies would find him attractive. At least his mind was on other things, and this goal was a worthy one.

On the sixteenth, I received a panicky letter from Cookie. The US newspapers were reporting that Dak Pek had been attacked, and now she knew that two of my camps were in trouble. The tone of my letters to her was always upbeat, and I tried never to concern her, but news of the war coming closer to me gave her great concern. I tried to address her worries:

> Dak Pek did get hit a week ago, and for a time it was problematic whether the camp would hold, but it did. Now everything seems to be in control, and the camp is no longer in danger. I don't want you to worry about me, because I am in Kontum, and that is far away from the fighting. I don't plan to volunteer to go into battle, and realistically my job pretty much guarantees that I can't volunteer. No one can do the job but me, and until a replacement is trained, I am safe in Kontum. I promise I will be in Hawaii in June and home on Sept. 15. Then we will have a big welcome-home party.

Things got testy in B-24 when interviews with Capt. Dave Cook from Dak Seang and Lt. Don Andrews from Dak Pek were published in *Stars and Stripes* and other civilian newspapers. Both Cook and Andrews were very derogatory in their descriptions of our LLDB (Vietnamese Special Forces) counterparts, as well as our ARVN allies. They described the LLDB as "thieves and cowards," among other adjectives, and this caused some angst at the Nha Trang headquarters. Col. Hennigan was later relieved because of his failure to maintain control of his troops, and Maj. Ramos was in one of the foulest moods I had ever seen. If I spotted him coming toward me, I ran the other way. Neither Cook nor Andrews was told they could not speak to the press, and the interviews were done in the respective camps, while the fighting was raging. The reporters got on helicopters and just flew out there. Those reporters were some crazy guys, but they got their stories. In retrospect, those interviews cost Col. Hennigan his chance to advance in rank and prompted an earlier-than-expected retirement.

Finally Capt. Strickler returned, and my job got a lot easier. I was still in charge of writing up the valor awards, but by that time the stack had gotten much smaller. Col. Hennigan received orders for his next assignment, and it would be teaching ROTC at Northwestern in Louisiana, only three hours from Lafayette. I had become very fond of him and was happy that we could continue our friendship after I was no longer part of the US Army.

This was the month when Prince Sihanouk was deposed and Long Nol took over. When this occurred, Cambodia turned from "neutral" to fighting to remove the communist influence from its borders. That signaled the beginning of the Cambodian campaign.

We had a company of Cambodian CIDG at Polei Kleng and a small contingent at Dak Seang. Somehow they found out that the coup was successful, and they wanted to go home to join the fight. The company from Polei Kleng was brought into Kontum and given to me; they were now, according to Col. Hennigan, "my Cambodes." He further ordered me to "pay and get rid of them."

Since that was all the direction I received and the colonel was still very pissed off at everyone because of the interviews, I had to come up with a plan on my own. I knew they wanted to go to Cambodia, but they couldn't just walk there.

I went to Pleiku to draw money to pay them, and while I was there, I met a pilot in the officers club. I was always gregarious, so I introduced myself and asked what he did.

"I fly for Air America." (This was a CIA-owned airline.)

"Really? What do you fly?"

"A DC3."

"Do you ever fly to Cambodia?"

"All the time."

"I have a load of Cambodes in Kontum that the colonel wants me to get to Cambodia. I am here drawing money to pay them. Can we make a deal?"

"Absolutely; just let me speak to your superior officer and get him to agree to hire me, and your Cambodes will be mine."

I brought him to my boss, the C-Team funds officer, went back to the bar, and left them to negotiate. I'm not sure what "closed" the deal, but a few minutes later, the pilot walked in.

"Bacque, we are set. Have my Cambodes at the Kontum airstrip tomorrow morning at ten o'clock. It will take two trips, over two days, so bring half tomorrow and the other half the next day."

I went back to Kontum, paid the troops, and, over the next two days, put them on the plane home. My task was accomplished, and both the colonel and the major were appreciative. It seems they had bigger fish to fry, and I was able to get them out of a jam. No one ever asked how I did it. We were expected to be creative in Special Forces; the outcome was important, not how it was achieved.

One morning the next week, at our morning briefing, the colonel asked, "Bacque, don't you speak French?"

"Not very well, sir; why do you ask?"

"The army is asking for French-speaking volunteers to fly with bird-dog pilots in Cambodia and help adjust artillery fire by speaking French to the Cambodian artillery batteries. Would you want to volunteer?"

"Sir, I have my hands pretty full just doing the stuff you want me to do, and flying over Cambodia isn't that appealing. Besides, my French is not that good, and I'm concerned that my miscommunication could have dire results."

"You're right; disregard the query."

I had dodged another bullet.

For the junior officers, the routine of garrison life was a bore, so for diversion, the pranks kept occurring. Randy Stroud seemed to bear the brunt of them. During his afternoon nap (we had a two-hour lunch break), Randy woke up to find a "flying rat" painted on his chest. The art was pretty good, but Randy didn't appreciate the skill of the artist. What upset him most was that he had slept through the deed. He gathered us all together that evening.

"I know one of you did this, and I want you to know that I'm pissed. I will find out who did it, and I will retaliate. Now I want each of you to draw a flying rat."

Evidently Randy thought that whoever had done the deed would draw a good likeness, and Randy would be able to catch him.

No one's rat looked anything like the one Randy still wore on his chest, and the perpetrator was never found—a mystery to this day.

And so April, the month that war finally came to us, was finally over. We had all survived, and for us in B-24, not much had changed.

# BEN HET

B-24 was responsible for six A-Camps located in Kontum Province: Polei Kleng, Dak Seang, Dak Pek, Mang Buk, Plateau Gi, and Ben Het. I had heard of Ben Het before I arrived because in February 1969, Russian tanks had attacked the camp, which made headlines in the States. At that time I was at Fort Bragg, just beginning my Special Forces training, and Ben Het was on everyone's lips.

The camp was located on Route 40, which was nothing more than a rutted dirt road leading into the borders of southern Laos and northern Cambodia, located about five miles west of the camp. The Ho Chi Minh trail snaked along those borders, and Route 40 was a main infiltration avenue into the Central Highlands. Ben Het was built just north on the road, with a pierced-steel planking runway lying on an east-west heading, just off the road. The camp itself was sitting astride two hills, one was occupied by the camp and the second, just to the west, was occupied by an artillery battery of 105 mm how-itzers, which seemed to fire around the clock. The artillery hill had taken the brunt of the earlier tank assault. The attack was disrupted by pinpoint artillery rounds fired directly at the tanks.

Ben Het A-Camp was located on the eastern hill. There was a trail leading from the airstrip, bordered by concertina wire, and ending at a gate, which led into the camp perimeter. The perimeter itself was perhaps half a mile long, cir-cling about halfway up the hill itself. Outside the perimeter was a cleared space that extended completely around the hill extending to the base. In the cleared area were antipersonnel mines as well as claymore mines. The perimeter itself was defined by several strands of razor-sharp concertina wire. About thirty feet from the wire was a string of fighting bunkers that extended completely around the hill. The Montagnards, who were the camp defenders, occupied these bunkers. The path from the airstrip continued up the hill, where another string of concertina defined the "American position," which covered the top of the hill. There was another gate at that perimeter and another much smaller perimeter of bunkers, manned by the A-Team.

On the crest of the hill were the living and command spaces, all under-ground but connected to the bunkers. There was a mess hall, manned by a Vietnamese cook and helpers, a shower area, which was aboveground, and a latrine, consisting of several wooden seats sitting above a fifty-five-gallon drum cut in half. Every week an indigenous crew would pull the drums out, pour diesel fuel in them, and light the fuel. The resulting blaze was suc-cessful in removing the contents, but the smell was something very hard to forget.

The tactical operation center, team room, and individual sleeping areas were reached by going down steps cut into the clay and reinforced with wood-en support. The sleeping areas were lined with cargo parachutes, which were in a camouflage pattern. These served several purposes. They did make the room a little more "homey" and also allowed the rats to cross the room on the silk, rather than across the floor. Several of the Americans had pellet pistols sent to them and used the rats for target practice.

The camp was continuously under sporadic mortar attacks, hence the need to live belowground. This was the norm for every A-Camp I visited, so I thought nothing of it when I first visited Ben Het in early November. I had arrived late in the afternoon, with the intention of spending the night. After dinner in the mess hall, I was told that the showers were on the very top of the hill, and I proceeded to them. The team sergeant told me that if I heard the sound of a mortar being shot to get my ass underground as soon as possible. As I climbed the hill in the gathering darkness, I thought I could see someone in the shower area. Since all the team members were still in the team area and only Americans were allowed to use the shower area, I was a little disconcerted. I had no weapon and felt very exposed. As I got closer, I saw that the person was a woman, taking a shower, which really concerned me. I immediately beat a hasty retreat back to the team room, reporting that I had seen a woman in the shower area. I was reassured that the lady was a friend of the camp commander, and she was there because he wanted her to be. Once again, I was amazed at how "special" Special Forces was. I thought that having camp followers had ended with the Romans.

Ben Het also figured, much later in my tour, into an attempt by Lt. Tom Cash and me to stamp out corruption. Tom was the camp funds officer, and he was in charge of paying the indigenous troops at the camp. All of the Americans knew that of the four to five hundred troops that were supposed to be at the camp, only two to three hundred actually were, but we paid the higher number. This was possible for several reasons. First, the indigenous people all looked alike to us, and we could not tell who had, and who had not, been paid. Second, almost none of them could write or sign their name, so we used an inked fingerprint to verify their pay. Third, at least one company was always in the field and would not be paid until they returned, so it was easy for a few extra—say fifty or so—of the troops to double-dip. This was done not for the benefit of the indigenous but for the benefit of our Vietnamese counterparts, who had a system for dividing the graft based on rank, ranging from Ben Het all the way to Nha Trang.

We knew what was going on, but we had no idea how to stop it. One day Tom and I were talking, and he said that he wanted to try something. When he paid the troops next, he would have the medic also give everyone a shot, and at that time, we would make a scratch on their thumbnail and place some ink on the scratch. The Vietnamese were told that this was a vaccine for highland streptococcus, a disease we made up. That way no one could come through the pay line twice because the ink on the scratch could not be removed. I thought the plan was ingenious and made sure I was at the camp when the plan commenced. We were able to pay only one company before we got a radio message from our headquarters in Nha Trang that we had to stop the process immediately. The reason given was that by scratching the fingernail, we were violating an old Montagnard belief that if we mutilated their bodies, their children would be born deformed. No one had ever heard of this fable, but it certainly ended our attempt to rectify a problem that we were disgusted by.

I complained to Col. Hennigan, but he said that even though he agreed with what we were attempting to do, the decision to stop was made far above his pay grade, and it was irreversible. This certainly shaded my perception of both our allies and the reason for us being in-country.

# PLATEAU GI

Copyright © 1998 Peter A. Bird

The most isolated A-Camp in the B-24 operational area was Plateau Gi. It was situated on the far-eastern edge of the Central Highlands, on a plateau where the mountains sloped to the sea. In fact, there were times when I believed I could see the South China Sea from the camp, but because it was over fifty miles away, I am sure it was my imagination.

Plateau Gi was the first camp in our area of operations that was turned over to the Vietnamese Special Forces; there were no Americans in residence there. But because the indigenous troops were still employed by the US government, I had to go there every month to distribute the payroll funds. At the other camps, there was always part of the troops on operations during pay time. But since I only came once a month to Plateau Gi, all troops were in camp, so they could be paid, but they could still pad the payroll records, as it was very easy for them to go through the line twice. Because I really knew no one at the camp, I had no idea who I was paying. They would just come up in a line and mark the pay sheet with a fingerprint. We always paid 100 percent of the camp.

The flight to Plateau Gi took almost an hour, and because of the remoteness of the camp, I usually had to spend at least a full day there every month. More than one time, either I was either weathered in or there was no available helicopter or bird dog that could pick me up, so on those occasions, I would have to spend the night. The camp was, like all the other camps in my area, populated by villagers whose families lived in close proximity. As was the case in most of the camps, Montagnard tribal members were the indigenous. At Plateau Gi, however, because it was so remote, the tribal members lived almost exactly as they had for the past hundred years or more. The men wore loincloths and carried crossbows. The women wore sarong-type skirts and went bare breasted. The women tended the fields and the children, while the men did the hunting and gathering. If a woman was pregnant, she would work in the fields until the birth was imminent, and then she would squat in a protected area adjacent to the field, have the baby, and return to work. The tribes lived in a communal setting, where everything belonged to the tribe and was shared. The women were uniformly attractive when they were teenagers but looked very old by forty. There were no water wells, stoves, or electricity, so the older women were in charge of bringing water from the nearby streams and firewood from the surrounding jungle. Water was carried in hollowed-out bamboo, with five to ten gallons carried at a time in a straw basket strapped to their backs. Firewood was also carried in the basket, adding fifty to sixty pounds per trip. The hills were very steep, and the women traversed the mud trails barefoot but seemingly with little effort. The older men helped the women in the field, but I never saw one carrying water or firewood; that was a woman's job. Both the men and women smoked "corncob" pipes, but I never saw any tobacco being grown, so there is no telling what herb was in the pipe. All of them chewed betel nut, so by their late twenties, their teeth—if any were left—were uniformly stained brown.

On my first visit, I watched the men hunting grasshoppers for fishing. This was accomplished by using long sticks to stun the grasshoppers, and then they were gathered up in a sack. A line of men walked through the tall grass, snapping the sticks and then bending down to retrieve the grasshoppers. I was amazed as I witnessed a task that had probably gone on for hundreds of years without change.

The camp also had a "crossbow factory," where they made crossbows for sale to chopper pilots and anyone else who visited the camp. I was considered somewhat a celebrity, since I brought their pay, so I was given a crossbow. I still have this gift to this day, and I treasure it.

Plateau Gi, maybe because it was so remote, never reported any action during the year I was there. Although we knew that there were VC and NVA in the area, there may have been an informal truce. The isolation, and lack of enemy activity, allowed me to really explore the natural beauty of the highland jungle and the primitive inhabitants who made it their home.

Because Plateau Gi had been turned over to the Vietnamese Special Forces, the Vietnamese A-Team commander was the camp commander; in this case it was a Montagnard major. This was unusual for several reasons. First, Montagnards were considered second-class citizens, and it was very unusual for one to become an officer at all, much less a major. Second, it was unusual for a major to be a camp commander; usually it was a captain. This major, whose name I do not recall, sat with me on an evening I was forced to stay over because of a weather problem. This occurred in late June 1969, shortly after the battles at Dak Pek and Dak Seang. During the battle for both camps, II Corps had sent in Vietnamese, regular army troops to help break the sieges. Those troops had performed poorly and often deserted the battlefield when faced with the enemy.

As we were having dinner, I asked the major, "Would you please explain something that has been troubling me for quite some time? The NVA troops that we are facing in this area are very well-disciplined fighters. They tie themselves to trees, chain themselves to machine guns, and strap mortars to their legs. They are prepared to, and in many situations do, fight to the death. And they are the invaders.

"The South Vietnamese troops, on the other hand, seem poorly trained, poorly disciplined, and seem to have no will to fight. This is their country, but they don't seem to want to protect it from the North. What is going on?"

He looked up, stopped eating, and, with a concerned look on his face, replied, "That is a very profound question and one I have grappled with as well. In my opinion there are several reasons. First, you Americans came here and told us that you would defeat the enemy, so we were relegated to defending our cities while you went on combat operations. Now you want us to take over and do what you felt we could not do. But that is not the main reason. The main reason is the difference in the two cultures. Our brothers in the north live in poor conditions, with rocky, barren soil. To live there takes a great deal of effort and will. We in the south have a very easy life. We just throw out the seeds and they grow; life is much easier. Our northern brothers see what we have, and they want it. We don't understand what we have, and we fail to protect it."

"Can we ever win this war?" I asked.

"One day, you Americans will be gone, and then I fear for our survival as a country. No, I do not think we can win this war."

I had gone to Vietnam as a hawk, truly believing that we were standing up to a communist menace by helping our ally in that fight. At that instant I became unsure, wondering if he was correct in his assertion that this war would never be won, that all the lives lost would have been in vain; I prayed that I would not be one of them.

Three and a half months to go.

# MAY 1970

After the excitement of April, it was nice to begin May in a much more relaxed environment. It appeared that the attacks on Dak Seang and Dak Pek had failed, and the invasion of Cambodia by US troops may have been a reason for the withdrawal of the attacking NVA forces. For whatever reason, peace seemed to return to Kontum Province.

But the pressure on Col. Hennigan and Maj. Ramos, from SF headquarters in Nha Trang, was really getting to them. My letter to Cookie on May 1 concerned this:

> I can't understand what the army does to guys. Both Col. Hennigan and Maj. Ramos have become completely irrational. An example is the plan to pay the troops this month. Because of the attacks on Dak Seang and Dak Pek, they want me to give them an alternative plan for scheduling the pay, which I did. Then they changed the plan at least ten times, and then finally agreed that my plan was best. I just don't know what is going on, but it is strange.

I flew out to Dak Pek on May 1, my first on-the-ground visit since the siege ended, and I was shocked. The camp was quiet but completely beat to hell. Jerry had been medevacked with malaria, but Don Andrews was still there. The biggest job they had before they could begin rebuilding was to clear the NVA bodies from the wire and the surrounding area and get them buried. A bulldozer was digging a mass grave, and Montagnards wearing masks were retrieving the bodies. The smell of death was everywhere.

Don gave me an NVA belt with a red star in the center as a souvenir. He said it belonged to an officer. I took it back to Kontum and gave it to John Ricci, who would be leaving soon to go back to the States. I suspected, rightly so, that I could get another sometime soon.

Rumor had it that the camp would be turned over to the ARVN Rangers in August, and the rebuilding had to be finished before that could happen; it didn't, and the camp was not converted until December.

On May 3, I delivered funds to Dak Seang and was amazed at how much better it fared than Dak Pek, even though it had been under siege for ten days more than Dak Pek. Dak Seang was also slated for conversion to the ARVN Rangers, and here the rebuilding was in full swing.

While I was there, a major general landed, walked around, asked some questions, and then got back in his chopper and left. No one seemed to know who he was or why he was there. We kidded that he would probably be awarded the Silver Star just for visiting; I don't know if that rumor was true.

May was also the beginning of the monsoon season, which helped cool the air but brought high humidity levels. Since I was from Louisiana, the humidity didn't bother me, but I heard complaints from others. That was also the month when Dak To, which had a large airfield and runway complex, came under attack, maybe by the same troops that had participated in the attacks on Dak Seang and Dak Pek. The attacks were not in strength, more like harassment, but were taken seriously by Second Field Force. A forward-operating command post was established at Tan Canh, just down the road from Dak To, and though SF had no operational control of the situation, Maj. Ramos sent me there to report back as to what was going on. He and the colonel did not want this action to become another black eye for them.

Because I was only a first lieutenant, the lowest-ranking officer in the FOB, Forward Operations Base, all I did was monitor the action and run errands for anyone senior to me—so everyone there. I couldn't wait to be relieved and return to Kontum. Finally, after three days, I was.

Cookie and I also started planning our R and R, which we hoped would happen in early June. One factor we did not count on was that June, because of school schedules, was one of the most requested months for R and R.

R and R was awarded based on time in-country. Even though I had been in-country for nine months, there were several people with longer in-country times, and they got first picks. Also, SF didn't have a lot of slots, and the best were kept and awarded to the Nha Trang headquarters; we got the rest. I wanted June 10 but got June 15. There were only so many days that I could go, as no one was trained to do my job but me, and I had to be in B-24 from the first of the month through the seventh or eighth and then again from the twenty-third to the end of the month. Even with that tight a window, I made it for June 15–21, six days in paradise with Cookie. Now we had a date to plan for and a diversion to keep us respectively busy. Of course, Cookie did the planning, and I did the agreeing.

One of the joys of camp life was the occasional "care package" sent from home, and the ones I received from South Louisiana were prized above all others. I would receive cakes, candies, Cajun delicacies, and all kinds of interesting and tasty treats. Maj. Ramos knew that I was always stocked with candy, and he had a sweet tooth. Often he would sneak into my office and help himself to the treats I had in containers on my desk. I knew he was the culprit because I had seen him surreptitiously leaving my office one evening, and the cap on the candy jar was not tightly sealed. I then decided to play a joke on him. I placed a cloth-covered spring in the jar, the kind that would leap out as you opened the container, scaring the crap out of the perpetrator. I then left my office and went to the club.

Later that evening he came in, and by the look on his face, I could tell he had been caught. He couldn't admonish me, as that would be tantamount to a confession. He knew I had outsmarted him this time.

He did make my life miserable for a few days, but it was well worth it. After that incident I gave him another nickname, "the gold leaf in the sky."

As the designated "utility player" in B-24, I never knew what task I may be given next. This time it was acting S-3 Air. This occurred because several of the captains were on R and R, and the job was not above my pay grade or intelligence level. It consisted of monitoring the helicopter assets assigned to us, keeping a log of their flights and telling them where to go and what to do based on instructions given to me by the S-3. The duty was interesting, and the pace helped the time pass quickly.

As soon as that duty ended, Capt. Strickler was sent to the field, and I again became acting S-1. One of my first duties was to coin the motto, "You fight; we write." I hoped every S-1 shop would adopt it, but of course it was ignored. All of B-24 got a big laugh out of my creativity; my humor wasn't always appreciated, but in this case it seemed to be.

I enjoyed the diversity that doing the different jobs presented, but the following is as I told Cookie in my letter:

I'm doing so many jobs that I'm beginning to feel like a rubber band; but I guess I am doing a good job, as they keep using me to fill in where needed.

Then I was again reassigned to hell, better known as the FOB at Tan Canh. This time I went to monitor radios, so at least I wasn't being sent on a fool's errand.

At this time, the FOB was commanded by, as I described to Cookie, a "Mad Russian Major" affectionately known as "Cement Head." I was never told where the nickname originated. But I further described him to Cookie as follows:

He's right out of the comic books. He looks the part of a Russian: swarthy in complexion and always with a five o'clock shadow. His hair is a short flattop, with the sides shaved to the skin. He speaks with a slight accent, and is always yelling at someone about something.

He has a system for everything, including a filing system that would put General Motors to shame, but nothing is operational. It sounds great on paper, but doesn't work in practice. The result is that you have three or four people talking on five radios at once, calling everyone in the world, and getting nothing done. It is pure chaos.

Then Randy returned from R and R and was sent out to take my place. After an hour of observing the action, he asked that I send him a gallon of tranquilizers from B-24 when I got back.

Since Randy was coming in "cold" and I did not have to return to B-24 immediately, I decided to spend another night at the FOB to both brief and prepare him for "Cement Head." But most of the time was spent with Randy regaling me with tales of Sydney. He had spent a wonderful time, met lots of comely lasses, and spent thousands of dollars. He described the trip as a "continuous leaflet drop of dollar bills over Sydney." His only complaint was that he had trouble sleeping because it was so quiet with no artillery sounds in the background, so he said he hired a hotel employee to beat on his door every hour or so, supposedly allowing him to sleep soundly. Whether or not this was the truth was never verified, but the story sounded good.

On my return to Kontum, I was assigned another task. This was more in keeping with my real job as funds officer, but it was, at times, heartbreaking. The job was to pay "death gratuities" to the family members of the CIDG killed at Dak Pek and Dak Seang.

I wrote this to Cookie:

One of the wives saw, while I was paying her, a picture on an ID card that I kept in his file. When she saw the picture she got emotional and asked if she could have it. She explained that she did not have a picture of her husband—this seemed to be the only one in existence—and it would mean so much to her to have it. I gave it to her, and she started crying. I felt so helpless. These people have been living with war for over twenty years; all they want is peace and a chance to live a stable life. They are simple people with a simple wish. This really tore me up; I had tears in my eyes.

A few days later, I was able to get Maj. Ramos again. Part of our daily routine was to take a malaria pill and write our name in the "pill book." Writing your name was considered more important than taking the pill, and the book was checked religiously. Maj. Ramos was not an early riser, and the pill book was closed at 7:30 a.m., when the mess hall closed. Since Maj. Ramos seldom was up that early, he started paying one of the ladies who worked in the mess hall to sign the book for him. One morning I saw her doing it and confronted her, and she told me the story. Although I thought this showed great initiative on the part of Maj. Ramos, I still felt compelled to share the tale with Col. Hennigan, who that evening awarded Maj. Ramos the boot award. Maj. Ramos and I were running neck and neck in the number of boots awarded, and any opportunity to get him the award was a joyous occasion for me. I am sure that, to this day, Maj. Ramos is wondering how his escapade was discovered. As a result, he did start rising earlier and signing in for himself.

On May 24, my orders for R and R finally arrived, scheduled for June 15 in Honolulu. Many of the men had already gone on R and R and were more than happy to share with me where to go and what to do. Even today, over forty years later, I remember how excited I was to be going and seeing Cookie again. We would be staying at the Hilton Hawaiian Village for six wonderful days; I couldn't wait.

But the work at B-24 still had to be done, and I was assigned another task. The colonel had obtained a document written in Vietnamese that he wanted translated and typed. I did not include in my letter to Cookie what was in the document, and I certainly do not remember, but I did describe the process to her:

> Randy and I were given the task of translating a document for the Col. Actually Jolys, my interpreter, is translating, and Randy and I are transcribing and typing. The problem is that Jolys is not sure of all the English words, so Randy and I are translating his translation. Basically, we have to decide what the document seems to be saying, and then make up our own interpretation. Then we have to type it, and neither of us knows how to type. Worse than that, Randy's spelling is atrocious, so when he is typing, I have to review and make corrections. It's almost like a committee trying to design a horse, and ending up with an elephant. We finally finished at 2:00 a.m. and gave it to Maj. Ramos for his review the next day. I thought he was going to make us redo the whole thing, but he just shook his head and told us what a terrible job we had done. Then he went off to give it to the Col. I guess he was OK, because we never heard a word from him.

I was scheduled to go to Plateau Gi on May 29 or 30 for my last time to pay, as the camp was being converted to ARVN control on June 1. Headquarters didn't want me to pay until the end of the month because they were afraid that the entire garrison would go AWOL as soon as I paid them. It appeared that the CIDG did not want to convert to ARVN control, but that was not my problem; once I paid them, my task was finished. I would miss going out there, as it was in a beautiful location, and when I went to the camp, as the only American there, I was treated almost royally. After this last trip, that adventure was over.

As the month ended, I was given another task, claims officer, which meant that I was the point person for all lost personal property belonging to the Americans at Dak Seang and Dak Pek. I had to take statements and file claim forms for all the team members. I told Cookie:

You'd be amazed at how much stuff some guys are claiming. I went out to both camps yesterday and got statements; now I have to type up the claim forms and submit them. How I wish I had taken typing more seriously in school.

And then, with that job behind me, May ended.

# JUNE 1970

June marked the beginning of my ninth month in Vietnam and my long-awaited R and R in Hawaii with Cookie. The war once more had faded away, and we were once again garrison-support staff. But as with all things military, if there was no war to fight, then a paperwork war was substituted. Col. Hennigan would soon be leaving, and one of the most important factors in a well-regarded departure was to have all the books in good shape. My fund reports were always impeccable, but the club books left something to be desired. So Maj. Ramos called me into his office.

"Lieutenant Bacque, you seem to know an awful lot about bookkeeping."

"Not really, sir; I just know how to add and subtract. Beyond that I get lost."

"You are much too modest. I have another job for you. Colonel Hennigan needs the books of the club to be beyond reproach, and my preliminary perusal tells me that this is not what we currently have. I need you to go through the books and make sure that anything of a questionable nature is resolved so that the colonel can go home without a worry. Understand?"

What I was hearing was code for *Make sure the books look good, even if they don't.*

"How far back do I need to go?"

"From when he took over B-24—ten months ago."

And I thought I could "coast" until R and R, less than two weeks away.

I'm not sure who was keeping the books, but I decided that my best course of action was to start from scratch and try to recreate what I believed, based on the major's request, would allow Col. Hennigan to leave country without a scandal. The sergeant major in charge of all the army clubs in-country had just been tried and convicted of embezzling hundreds of thousands of dollars, and no commander was being allowed to leave country without a departure audit. That audit would occur while I was on R and R.

I remembered from my first assignment as club officer, before I became the funds officer, that there was a significant fund balance due to an illegal dice game that was ended before either Col. Hennigan or I arrived. We had been whittling away at that balance by having the club pay for the mama-sans who cleaned our rooms and did our laundry. The club fund also paid for our meals in the mess hall, and Col. Hennigan had even suggested that it could be used to purchase Rolex watches for the men. That idea went by the wayside and was never implemented, but we still had a significant fund balance. Explaining the origin of the fund balance, as well as the use of scraps of paper in the cash box purporting to explain the inflows and outflows, was what I was chosen to fix. Maj. Ramos knew we had a problem, and I was volunteered to repair it.

Although I did not tell Cookie how I did it and I do not remember, I did tell her that I reconstructed the books and that Col. Hennigan passed his termination audit with no discrepancies.

Cookie, I met with Maj. Ramos the night before the audit and showed him my work—the discrepancies I had found, as well as how I rectified them. He was most appreciative and told me I had done a wonderful job. I am starting to wonder if anything that the army is depending on has any real veracity. It is so easy to build something from nothing, and as long as it "balances," it is then gospel.

But the mission of getting the colonel home with no "demerits" was the job I was given and the job I did, even though real accounting was a course I'd barely passed.

One of my OCS classmates, Jesse Roland, was assigned to FOB Two, the forerunner of today's Delta Force. Their mission was supersecret, and most of their activity was cross border, but in much larger units than the C and C units, which usually were six- to eight-man teams. Jesse's unit was in Kontum for a mission that he could not share with me, but we were able to visit. I briefed him on the other guys we knew and what gossip I had regarding them. Jesse's unit was later involved in a mission called Tailwind just as we were leaving country, and I remember Jesse being so concerned that he wasn't there with them. If he could have left Cam Ranh Bay and rejoined the unit, he would have. As for me, I just wanted on the plane to go home, but that was three months down the road.

On June 11, I was able to leave for Pleiku and then Nha Trang carrying my fund reports. I was planning to spend a few days there and then leave for R and R on the afternoon of the fifteenth. While in Pleiku, I discovered that a voucher I had approved for a party to celebrate the conversion of Plateau Gi to a Ranger camp was, according to regulations that I misread, not authorized. Had the voucher gone to Nha Trang, it would have been disallowed, and I would have owed the money, about two hundred dollars. When this was pointed out to me, I immediately changed the voucher from Plateau Gi to Dak Pek, and since Dak Pek wasn't being converted, a party was OK. I guess, in retrospect, what I did was wrong, but the money had been spent on a party, I didn't get any of the funds, and I didn't think that I should be penalized for a stupid rule. I guess my Louisiana upbringing made me a perfect person for the jobs I was given.

On the afternoon of June 15, 1970, at 4:00 p.m., my plane left Cam Ranh Bay and arrived in Hawaii at 2:00 p.m. that same afternoon. How could you arrive at a place ten hours away and get there before you left? No complaints; I was happy to be there.

As we in-processed, we were warned about the possibility that our wives/girlfriends might have had a change of heart. I wasn't even listening; I was looking for Cookie in the crowd around the bus. I didn't see her and was wondering where she was when she jumped on my back. It was great to see her, and I couldn't wait to get her to the Hilton Hawaiian Village, the hotel we had booked.

At first it seemed that the six days stretching ahead was forever, but they did fly past. One remarkable coincidence was that when we were in the elevator one afternoon, we were joined by members of the Million Dollar Round

Table, who were holding their annual meeting in Hawaii. I remember being awed because even back then, I knew these were the best of the best—in my mind the Green Berets of the life-insurance industry. That I would one day join that industry and become a member of that elite organization was not something I even considered as a possibility that afternoon.

And then it was over, and I flew back to Vietnam. I told Cookie in my next letter:

> The flight back to Vietnam seemed much too short, and was so quiet.
> I guess everyone was content with their memories and chose not to
> break the spell.

At B-24 my job was waiting. It was time to start the payroll cycle, so I dove back in. But something subtle was happening between Maj. Ramos and me. All of a sudden I started getting to know him and, horror of horrors, to like him. When I got back from R and R, he sat with me in the bar and started telling me about his life, his career, the many places he had been, and the fun he'd had in his career. I relayed the following to Cookie:

> I'm starting to think that he is a cool guy. He's really a romantic at
> heart and does some neat things when he and his wife are on trips.
> For example, he sends flowers to his hotel room; I might need to try
> that next time.

As June ended, my time in the army dropped to less than three months. I had R and R in Hong Kong planned for July, and then just the month of August would be left; by September 1, I would be training my replacement and getting ready for home. What had seemed so distant nine months prior seemed now to be just around the corner.

# JULY 1970

**N**ow with June behind me, I officially became a short-timer. I had less than three months left on my tour: seventy-six days, to be exact. I was still basking in the glow of my Hawaiian R and R and planning my next one, to Hong Kong. Life at B-24 returned to the daily routine of army life behind the lines. Packages from home, movies at night, and occasional floor shows helped allay the boredom. As usual, the first week of the month was filled with busy-work, getting the fund reports in and my reports out. We had a muted Fourth of July celebration, but most of my effort was directed in getting information on Hong Kong, as my seven-day leave was scheduled to start on July 8.

Then I ran into an old acquaintance from my LSU days, Sgt. Jim Brock, in Pleiku. He had come into country at the same time I did, and we had gone through in-country orientation together. He was assigned to the Kontum Mike Force and was in Pleiku for some stand-down time.

"Brock, how are you doing?"

"Fine, Lieutenant, just killing some time; I'm getting ready to go to Hong Kong."

"Really? So am I. When are you scheduled?"

"Sometime next week; my orders are fluid."

"Well, I am scheduled for the eighth. Why don't we go together?"

"Sounds fine to me. Let me check with admin and get back to you."

"Come see me at B-24, and let me know," I said.

"OK."

On July 6, Brock appeared at my office door. "Hey, Lieutenant, I'm in. Let's make plans."

Both of us had been talking to plenty of people and had some great information on Hong Kong. We knew that the best way to go would be commercial, and the cost was only $130 round-trip from Saigon, but both of us were cheap and hoping to get on a free R and R flight. We were in the middle of the rainy season, which made in-country travel more difficult, but it also showed me the marvelous growing power of jungle vegetation. In December the road to Pleiku was cleared for one hundred yards on either side to help thwart ambushes. It obviously had worked, as I drove the road at least once a week with no problem. Now I wrote Cookie:

> The road has stayed clear from December to just a few weeks ago. Today on my drive the bushes are ten to twelve feet high, right up to the side of the road. This vegetation grows like wildfire.

On July 7, Jim and I planned to leave Kontum, heading for Saigon, but the weather did not cooperate. We missed our flight to Saigon, but we were finally able to get to Pleiku that afternoon. The only flight leaving Pleiku that afternoon was to Da Nang, but it was delayed in arriving, and instead of Da Nang, it went to Cam Ranh, arriving at midnight. There we were assigned a new crew and left for Da Nang at 1:30 a.m., arriving at 3:00 a.m. The terminal was shut down and there was no transportation, so we slept on the floor until 8:30 a.m., when the terminal opened. We were able to catch a ride to the R and R center, where we learned that a flight would be leaving for Hong Kong the next day, but our chances of getting on it were slim, since we were going on leave, not R and R. We decided to stick around anyway and caught a ride to the Special Forces compound, where we planned to spend the night. This also allowed us to get travel orders cut for Saigon, in case we were unsuccessful in getting on the R and R flight. Then we went to the local branch of Chase Manhattan Bank to buy some traveler's checks, something that had been so simple at home. Here they needed to verify our identity and our travel orders, so they insisted on calling Kontum to make sure we were who we said we were. Well, phone service between Kontum and anywhere is very problematic, and I told them so, but to no avail. Four hours later they agreed to give me $500 in traveler's checks. I wanted $1,000, but they told me that I should consider myself lucky to get what I got. Then it was back to the R and R center, where we were told that the original "slim chance" was a little better, but not much. We decided to take our chances. We should have stayed in the SF compound, where at least we would have had AC and mosquito nets. But we didn't, and we paid for it.

The next morning our worst fears were realized: the plane was full, and no other flights were scheduled until next week. Well, we had our travel orders for Saigon, so we hitched a ride on the next plane heading south, hoping our luck would change. But now we had a new member of our group, a helicopter pilot heading for Hong Kong as well. We landed in Saigon at 3:00 p.m., got to the R and R center at 3:30 p.m., and found out that the next R and R flight to Hong Kong was two days away. All of a sudden the $130 commercial flight looked great. We were told the next flight left at 4:30 p.m., and we might be able to make it. So we bummed a ride in a jeep to the terminal at Tan Son Nhut, getting there at 4:25 p.m., but we were not allowed on the flight. We were allowed to buy tickets for the next morning's flight, leaving at 7:00 a.m.

So we went back to the R and R center, where we were given a room with AC in the transient officers' quarters. Jim, being enlisted, went to his quarters, with an agreement to meet after a shower and a change into civvies. Our plan was to explore the airbase attached to the R and R center. While waiting for Jim to return, I ran into Vernon Alford, a Louisia native and graduate of Northeastern in Monroe, who had gone to OCS with me. He was just returning from his second trip to Hawaii and brought me up to date on his experiences. He was assigned to the Twenty-Fifth Infantry Division, and his company commander was Capt. Yoshita, our old OCS CO. That must have been a shocker to both of them.

When Jim returned, he told us that his room had no AC, so we decided that he would sleep in the officers' bunkroom with us. Who would know?

Then it was off to the airbase, where we had dinner and a drink in the "O" club—Jim was never asked to prove his status. But it was the airbase itself that amazed us all. There was even a base laundry, so, since Jim and I would be wearing civvies in Hong Kong, we left our dirty field-dress uniforms to be laundered in our absence, planning to pick them up on our return.

I described it to Cookie this way:

You wouldn't believe the airbase; it seemed just like home—a piece of the US, transported over here. They have sidewalks, an indoor movie theater, and so many snack bars, including even a Mexican snack bar. Anyway, we were like country boys on our first visit to the city, amazed at all we saw.

After supper we took in a Woody Allen movie, and then went back to the Batchelor Officers Quarters, where we proceeded with our plan to sneak Jim in; we all spent the night in comfort.

Tomorrow, Hong Kong.

# HONG KONG

The trip over was uneventful, except for the landing. It appeared that we were first going to crash into some buildings and then land in the water. I heard later that landing in Hong Kong was a challenge to even the most skillful pilots. It certainly appeared that way to me. It was noon Hong Kong time, so we had a whole afternoon to check out the surroundings.

We checked into the Park Hotel, where Jim and I agreed to share a room at a cost of seven dollars each—not bad. The room had two single beds, adequate AC, and a view of the building next door, but what can you expect for seven dollars? The doorman immediately offered to bring some girls up for us, but Jim and I demurred. We were there to shop and had our girls waiting at home.

That first afternoon was dedicated to shopping for camera gear. I had already decided that I wanted a Nikon camera and lenses. I ended up getting a complete outfit including a carrying case for $450, a great bargain even by Hong Kong standards. The only problem was that all I had in traveler's checks was $500, so that left me a little short of cash. I had been told that certain places would accept personal checks, but negotiating that on top of trying to get the best price made bargaining difficult. In my shopping priorities, the camera was first, but number two was a gold Rolex. and that would prove a challenge, since I needed three: one for Dave Cook, one for Bob Lockhart, and one for me, but I knew I would figure that all out.

Jim and I both had studied about Hong Kong and knew what we wanted to do. We rode to the top of Mount Victoria, ate in the floating restaurant, crossed on the Star Island Ferry, had tea in the Peninsula Hotel, took a bus to the Chinese border, shopped in the China Fleet Store, and did everything that tourist books suggested, but mostly we bought things. I even bought Cookie a mink stole for $200, using a personal check and my military ID, that we still have today. All in all, Hong Kong was a great success, and we left with fond memories.

As it was in Hawaii, at first you seem to have so much time, and before you know it, the trip is over. But the excitement didn't end because the trip home was very eventful. We left Hong Kong just before Typhoon Ruby hit, and the trip back to Saigon was very rough. When we arrived in Saigon about 4:00 p.m., we found that the laundry had lost our uniforms, so we had to finish our trip in our civvies, not as easy as it sounds. We were booked on a flight to Cam Ranh, arriving at 7:00 p.m., and there the fun started, as everyone needed to hear why we were in civvies, and we had to show proof, including IDs and orders, to allow us to proceed.

We left for Pleiku at 9:00 a.m. but could not land because of weather, so we diverted to An Khe. There we were scheduled on another flight to Pleiku, leaving at 1:00 a.m. That flight actually left at 2:30 a.m., but it also could not land at Pleiku, so they diverted back to Cam Ranh, landing at 4:00 a.m. in a destination we had left nine hours earlier. At 9:00 a.m. we left for Pleiku again, this time landing successfully. But then we were told that our flight to Kontum was canceled, so we were sent in a truck convoy. Jim and I, still wearing civvies and having no weapons, rode in the back of a truck.

About halfway between Pleiku and Kontum, the truck pulled off the road with two flat tires, and we were stranded for an hour while they were fixed. I was very nervous, as on this particular stretch of road, a road I traveled often, four members of CCC, Command and Control Central, a secret cross-border operation run by SF, had been ambushed the month before, and three of the four were killed. The fourth got away by sprinting to a cyclo and leaping onboard in a hail of bullets. A cyclo was motor scooter with a body attached. It could hold four to six people comfortably but often held up to ten or twelve. This was cab transportation between Pleiku and Kontum.

Sitting in the back of that truck with no weapon made me very anxious.

Finally the flats were fixed, and we proceeded to B-24. By the time we got to Kontum, Jim and I had been up for over thirty-six hours, so we were bushed. I answered questions about my lack of uniform, read my mail, and then went straight to bed.

# RICKY

But the excitement was not over because on July 19, a few days after I returned from Hong Kong, my roommate Roger returned from a trip to the headquarters in Nha Trang carrying a mail sack. I asked him what was in it, and he replied, "Take a look." I did and almost had a heart attack. Coiled in the sack was a twelve-foot Burmese python in a bad mood.

"Roger, what in the hell are we going to do with the snake?"

"It will be a pet; a friend of mine was leaving country and had no one to leave it with, so I told him we would take care of it."

"Where will we keep it?"

"I was thinking we could get the carpenter to build a cage for it and keep it in the bathroom."

"What about food?"

"My buddy said to just buy a live chicken or duck once a week, and it will do fine."

"Does it have a name?"

"No, but who is the biggest snake we have at B-24?"

"Major Ramos?"

"Right. We will name him Ricky, and he will never know why."

"What a great idea."

We brought the snake, in the bag, to the carpenter the next morning. We were forced to do so because the mama-san who cleaned our room refused to come back after she looked into the bag. A few days later, Ricky's cage was finished, and he moved into our bathroom. We would occasionally let him out of the cage, and he would climb the wall and look in the mirror, an activity he never tired of.

The small officers club was just down the covered veranda from our rooms, and one day, just after he arrived, we decided to bring Ricky in for a visit. A young Montagnard lady named Chut tended the bar, and she was on duty. We carried Ricky in with his body hidden by the bar and set him on a barstool. He slowly raised his head above the bar and saw the mirror, which intrigued him. Chut was polishing glasses with her back to the bar and did not notice Ricky's arrival. When Ricky saw his reflection in the mirror, he hissed, which was the first indication to Chut there was an alien presence. She saw the snake's head in the mirror, turned toward us with a horrified scream, and in one leap cleared the bar and exited the room. Because she refused to come back in, and because both Col. Hennigan and Maj. Ramos, who walked in shortly after this occurrence, wanted to be served, Roger, Ricky, and I were confined to quarters for the remainder of the evening, and Roger and I had to pull extra duty for several weeks. Ricky was forgiven.

Ricky became a camp mascot, and on feeding day a large contingent would gather as he captured and consumed either a duck or chicken. We fed him weekly, and you could see the bulge in his body work its way down the chute. By the end of the week, he would become ill tempered, and that was an indication that he was hungry. After feeding, though, he was docile and would roam our rooms, never causing trouble. Because of that we became complacent, and one day he vanished. We wondered how he could have escaped, but he was nowhere to be found. One afternoon, several days later, as I entered my room, I heard a sound, and I looked up. Ricky was staring at me. He had worked himself into the concrete blocks at the top of the wall, which were placed with the open areas facing in and out of the room. This was done for ventilation, and there was a screen covering the opening. Ricky had "woven" himself in and out of several of the blocks. When I attempted to pull him out, he showed quite a bit of displeasure and would not budge. Roger and I tried numerous methods of extracting him, all to no avail. Our task was made more difficult because Ricky was woven into blocks that were nine to ten feet up in the air. Finally, growing frustrated and not wanting to leave him there (in case he decided that night to repay us for the agony we were putting him through), I stumbled on a solution. We had a broom in the room, and I decided to light it on fire and place the flame in close proximity to Ricky's tail. It worked; Ricky quickly exited his lair and was easily captured.

Ricky remained a camp fixture until Roger left, several months after I did. About two years later, Roger came to visit me in Louisiana, and I inquired about Ricky. Roger had heard from his replacement that shortly after he had left country, the Vietnamese ate Ricky. The report was that since Ricky had consumed so much fowl during his life, he tasted just like chicken.

But July brought sorrow as well because Col. Hennigan's tour of duty ended, and Col. Venn replaced him. I had grown very fond of Col. Hennigan, and I believed he felt the same about me. His last night in camp was a rip-roaring drunk. I told Cookie in my letter:

The party was really bad. Everyone got wiped out, and if the VC had wanted to, they could have practically walked into the compound without firing a shot. I guess we're real lucky that Kontum is "pacified."

As with any new commander, Col. Venn took some getting used to. The main difference in style was his attitude toward our Vietnamese counterparts. Col. Hennigan had always been gracious and treated them with great respect. I had kind feelings at first as well, but they had changed. The main reason was what had happened at Ben Het, Dak Seang, and Dak Pek and my belief that our people were dying needlessly. I am sure Col. Hennigan had the same feelings, but his gracious attitude toward the LLDB never wavered. Col. Venn, on the other hand, was by nature distrustful and brusque, an attitude that suited me better at that time.

About that time, Bob Lockhart showed up to claim his Rolex. He had been in Bangkok on R and R and had some tales to tell. But first he had to withstand a blistering attack from Maj. Ramos, who ordered him to explain why he had been gone two weeks for a one-week R and R. I am not sure of the final resolution, but Bob looked like a whipped puppy when he emerged from the major's office.

On July 20 I received my DEROS orders. I would be leaving on September 15, flying to Fort Lewis, Washington, and since I would have less than ninety days of obligation remaining, I would be discharged at that time. Wonderful news, and only fifty-seven days to go. But there was still my job, so I picked up my funds in Pleiku, but because of the CCC ambush, I was not allowed to drive by myself with Jolys, which was fine with me. I had to wait for a convoy and join up with them. When a serviceman got "short" (meaning he didn't have much time left in-country), he got cautious, so none of the extra precautions bothered me. Just two more funds cycles, and I was through. I began to wonder who my replacement would be. And with that thought, July ended.

# AUGUST 1970

There seemed to be no perceptible change with the start of this new month, other than the restriction on traveling the road to Pleiku alone. As soon as I finished my fund reports and was ready to deliver them, Jolys and I found a convoy leaving in the early morning. We joined in and merrily proceeded down the road to Pleiku. About halfway there, we heard the sound of small-arms fire and immediately pulled to the side of the road and took up defensive positions in the roadside ditch. We had no idea what was going on up the road, but the gunfire finally stopped, and about thirty minutes later, the convoy started to slowly move again. About a quarter of a mile down the road, we passed about five bodies from the ambush party who had made the mistake of firing on our column. The bodies looked to be those of teenagers dressed in local peasant garb, surely not NVA. Why they had decided to take on our convoy was never answered, and their fighting days were certainly at an end. That was the first and last time I witnessed the enemy up close, and that was fine with me.

We would routinely receive rocket attacks that never caused us anxiety because they never landed in close proximity to our camp. We all believed that "Luke the Gook" was just shooting at us to keep us on our toes. But when you start to get short, even the misses can cause anxiety.

One afternoon, just about "club time," the sirens went off, and we moved to our bunkers, where we were more protected. We could actually see the rockets pass over our position, impacting harmlessly outside the perimeter. Before the all-clear siren sounded, I went to my room because I felt the call of nature. I had no concern that Luke's aim would improve, and I had my own deposit to make. Just then a terrific explosion went off, seemingly just outside my room. As I tried to process what was happening, I decided Luke had zeroed in on the compound and that the next rocket would be in my room. I have never been good at multitasking, and trying to wipe myself, put on my flak jacket and steel pot, and reach for my M-16 was far beyond my limited abilities, but knowing that the next rocket was on the way gave me superhuman abilities. In just a few seconds, I was diving into the bunker, trailing toilet paper behind me. My bunker mates found that to be amusing. They informed me that the explosion had been caused by a perimeter claymore that seemed to be struck by lightning. Both had exploded at the same time, giving extra volume to the claymore blast. Those still in the bunker found my reaction hilarious. Although I was not awarded a "boot" award, a new award was decided upon. I was the first, and probably the last, recipient of the "dirty ass" award.

In my letter to Cookie on August 6, I wrote the following:

At this time it still feels like a fantasy to me that I will be home in thirty-nine days. Time here passes day by day, and all I have to look forward to is the next day with a letter from home or a newspaper. It's really a meaningless existence. Last night I really started to think about going home and imagining how great that would be.

I imagine first getting on a plane at Cam Ranh Bay and knowing that I'd never have to see this country again; then getting off the plane in Fort Lewis and knowing that I'd never have to be in the army again; and then getting off the plane in New Orleans and knowing that I'd never have to be away from you again. I could almost feel myself at home, and the feeling was wonderful. The time is getting so short, yet seems so long. Well, only thirty-nine more days, and my dreams will be reality.

On the eleventh I hand-carried my funds reports to Nha Trang and spent four days there because Maj. Ramos wanted me to attend a meeting on his behalf. I did not tell Cookie what the meeting involved, and I don't remember, but I was still the "utility" guy at B-24. Everyone seemed to think, if you can't or don't want to go, send Bacque. But what the hell, Nha Trang was not the boonies, and a lot of my friends were there, as well as beaches and booze, both of which I was partial to.

I wrote to Cookie on August 15—I had no time to write while in Nha Trang—and told her the following:

After a four-day drunk in Nha Trang, I am really happy that in just a month I will be a civilian and will have more to do than just drink.

But before that could happen, we had to bid Maj. Ramos adieu, another cause for celebration. All jokes aside, I was actually sorry to see him go. I have learned that all of us have different leadership styles, and Col. Hennigan's appealed to me more than the major's, but in his own way, Maj. Ramos was as good a leader as Col. Hennigan. It just took me longer to realize it.

August 18 was Maj. Ramos's going-away party, and by the looks of him, he was not going to remember anything. It was also the day that Roger and I who had started brewing rice wine in our bathroom found out that the recipe was working. We had the medic check the alcohol content, and it was fifty proof, heading for one hundred. I don't remember what precipitated the brewing—probably we did it just because we could—but I did tell Cookie that it didn't taste too bad. I never mentioned it in any other letters, so we either drank it all or threw it away.

I still had my funds job, and now I wasn't too excited about taking the funds to the camps in the helicopters. Since I was short, I wanted to stop taking chances that I had never thought about before. But soon I would have my replacement, and in just a few weeks, I'd see Cookie face-to-face again.

# SEPTEMBER 1970: GOING HOME

As September started, it seemed surreal. Could it really be true that I was going home? Although I never doubted that I would survive both the country and the war, there was always that little nagging feeling. And so I did become more cautious. I actually took a chopper to Pleiku to pick up my last funds delivery. With me was my replacement, Lt. Jeff Gaab. He was smart and a quick learner, so I had no concern about his ability to continue my stellar performance. My first words of instruction were, "You have two safes; use them both."

On September 7, I left for Nha Trang, with more than a week left for DEROS. But no one complained, and I wanted to be there when Bill Brooks left country. And I also wanted to partake in the booze and luxury of the head-quarters compound. There was the beach, snorkeling equipment, and even water-skiing. Not bad for a war zone.

The night before Bill left, we had a commode-hugging drunk. One of the guys had a bottle of Korean root wine that he had chanced upon, and after a full night at the club, we drank that. I can honestly say that even to this day, the taste and aftereffects of the drinking are still a vivid memory, and I have no desire to ever taste the brew again.

The next morning, with the worst hangover I can remember, I bade Bill good-bye. Unbeknownst to me, he had a tailored set of jungle fatigues made, and he looked like John Wayne as he walked out of the office to his transpor-tation. I was sorry to see him go but happy that he had made it. Now I just had to wait for Bowley and the rest of the crew to show up, but I knew that it was only a matter of days until we all walked through the gates as well, on our way home.

On September 13, our last scheduled day in Nha Trang, we started drinking in the club in the early afternoon. By evening all of us were dropping syllables and speaking incoherently. I had always been a bit of a ham, and I decided to impersonate Lt. William Calley, who had just been arrested for the My Lai massacre. I stood on top of the table, and as I started my monologue, which had everyone in hysterical fits of laughter, a very upset major came and confronted me.

"What in the hell do you think you're doing, Lieutenant?"

"What does it look like to you, sir?"

"Making an ass of yourself and disrespecting my army."

"Sir, tomorrow I leave for home, and when I get to the States, I become a civilian, so basically I don't care about your sensibilities. I'm out of here."

He glared at me, and I glared back, but he left, and I shut up; we both won.

That evening, John Hale, one of the people who had gone through OCS with us and had gone on to flight school, came into the bar. He had just recently arrived, and we were happy to see him. He asked about our transport to Cam Ranh Bay for the next morning, and we told him we had no idea of what had been arranged.

"Guys, don't worry; just show up at the chopper pad at nine, and I will fly you there."

Without giving any thought to the fact that we would be traveling with no authorization and going to a place where we were not expected, we immediately accepted.

The next morning John flew us to Cam Ranh and dropped us at the helipad. The only problem was that no one knew we were coming, and the helipad was in the middle of nowhere. One of the guys said, "No sweat; I'll find us transportation," and left.

Soon he returned, driving a school bus he had found sitting with keys in the ignition. We loaded our gear and started searching for the repo depot where we had to report in order to get our flight assignments for home. Of the sixteen who had reported over, fifteen of us were going home.

Now the CS (chickenshit) started, but we were so happy to be leaving that almost nothing they did could faze us. We had lectures that afternoon and were told that there was a flight leaving at midnight flying through Yokota and on to Oakland. The next one left the following morning; it went through Okinawa and then on to Fort Lewis. It made no difference which flight we were on because all of us were getting discharged wherever we arrived, but we did want to fly back together.

We went to the club to drink and wait. At midnight they announced that Bowley and several others would be on the Yokota flight; the rest of us would be leaving in the morning. The club closed at midnight, so we went to bed, ragging Bowley and his group for deserting us. They saluted with one finger and joyfully left, only to return again at 2:00 a.m., as there had been a mistake. We would be going together.

The next morning, terribly hungover, we all boarded the freedom bird and took off about 9:00 a.m. There was an enormous howl of delight when the wheels left the pavement. We arrived at Fort Lewis the same day we left, at 7:00 a.m. I still couldn't fathom how you could fly halfway around the world and still arrive before you left, but then again, I went to LSU.

We were fed, paid, and given our discharge orders. Then we left for the Seattle airport, about sixty miles away. There was a flight to Dallas leaving in ninety minutes, and I told the cab driver if he got me there in time to catch it, I had a $100 tip for him. We made the trip in less than an hour, plenty of time to catch the flight.

Since I was an REMF, I was not carrying any souvenirs, but several of the guys had SKS rifles they were hand-carrying. As we exited the cab, we commandeered two luggage carriers and ran through the airport to my gate; they wanted to make sure I either got on the flight or stayed with them in the bar.

Back then we traveled standby using our orders to access the planes. If there was room, you got on board; if not, you stayed. The gods were with me because I not only got on board but also was given a seat in first class. How lucky was that? I changed in Dallas and arrived in New Orleans at 6:00 a.m., greeted at the gate by Cookie and my brothers. After a year away, it felt great to be home.

# EPILOGUE

I came home luckier than most, seemingly unmarked in body, mind, and spirit but still changed. I was disillusioned. But I still had a living to make, a wife to support, and a life to live.

I thought I wanted to be a stockbroker, but no one was hiring, so I took a job selling life insurance as a temporary position, one that I have remained in for over forty-three years. I was able to devote myself to both growing my practice and being active in the community. In the back of my mind, I believed, and still do, that politics causes war. Furthermore, we just don't elect the best and brightest to political office because they don't offer themselves. I pledged to rectify that perception.

As my practice and reputation grew, I moved toward politics, actually being elected to the Louisiana House of Representatives in 1987. I stayed close to Col. Hennigan, who retired to a farm in north Louisiana. Unfortunately, shortly before I was elected, Col. Hennigan died, still a young man, from lung cancer. I think he was one of the first casualties of Agent Orange, a toxin that would affect my body in 2004. Luckily it was prostate cancer, caught early and seemingly cured.

What caused me to change from an excited second lieutenant, eager to go to war, into a disillusioned first lieutenant, eager to shed the uniform? That was the question posed to me by my friend Carl Bauer, who encouraged me to tell this story.

My disillusionment was born out of a disappointment in the army system and the anguish it was causing in the ranks. I will cite several examples, all of which I touched on in my story.

The first had to do with valor awards. Since I was the principal author of the awards for B-24, I knew the system. The commander on the ground recommends all awards. He is the only one to witness acts of bravery, and his recommendation is based on that premise. There were several times when the recommendation of the ground commander was ignored, not to give a lesser award but a more prestigious one. In one particular case, a camp commander was recommended for an Army Commendation Medal, with V (valor) device; it came back a Silver Star.

Another occurred when Capt. George Dooley was sent to Dak Seang, in the very first hours of the siege. He went in because Col. Hennigan was concerned that the camp commander might not be a strong enough leader. Despite that fact, the camp commander was recommended for a Silver Star, along with all other participants.

I heard, but cannot verify, that the Silver Star given to the camp commander was upgraded to a DSC, the second-highest valor award, while Dave Cook, the executive officer, who according to Capt. Dooley should have received the Medal of Honor, had his Silver Star downgraded to a Bronze Star with Valor. George Dooley also received a Bronze Star with Valor, but not a Silver Star.

Col. Hennigan also flew into Dak Seang under heavy fire, and to the best of my knowledge, he was never recommended for a valor award.

After the battle ended, several colonels were flown to the top of Nui Ek and walked down into the camp. Not a shot was fired, but I heard they had been put in for Silver Stars. Seeing this happen should make anyone question the integrity of the system, and it did much to discourage me.

The second issue was the corruption that occurred in the ranks of our allies and the seeming indifference of our headquarters to it. We loved our indigenous troops, and they loved us. But they had to be disillusioned at our allowing the LLDB to continually extort monies from them. But worst of all, the selling of supplies upset us—me—the most. During the sieges of Dak Seang and Dak Pek, the airdropped supplies were given to the LLDB to distribute to the CIDG. We found out later that the LLDB were selling those supplies, not distributing them. This is what caused Dave Cook and Don

Andrews to give blistering interviews to *Stars and Stripes* and other publications, interviews that probably cost Dave Cook his Silver Star and certainly cost Col. Hennigan his career. For our commanders to allow this to happen, with seeming indifference, was decisive for me.

And finally, it was the shooting of the MACV advisors by our allies that completely sent me over the edge. I heard it on the radio, so it was not rumor; it is fact. I heard those two men go off the air and can only imagine what actually happened to them.

So I came back changed, but not shattered. I still believe that Vietnam was a crucial part in helping me become who I am.

And I was lucky that my Vietnam was "A Walk in the Park."

# Glossary

**4.2 Mortar:**    4.2-inch diameter mortar, the largest in our arsenal

**Airborne:**    Parachutist, those who jump from an aircraft with parachutes

**AIT:**    Advanced Individual Training

**ARVN:**    Army of the Republic of South Vietnam

**AWOL:**    Absent without leave

**B-40:**    A communist, handheld, rocket-propelled grenade launcher

**Basketball:**    An American aircraft flare ship

**Bird Dog:**    A forward air controller, usually flying a small single-engine plane

**C-7:**    Caribou, a cargo plane able to land and take off on short runways

**CAPO:**    Civic Action/Psychological Operations

**CIDG:**    Civilian Irregular Defense Group, the hired troops at our A-Camps

**CO:**    Commanding Officer

**COC:**    Combat Orientation Course

**DEROS:**    Date Estimate Return from Overseas, the date a soldier is scheduled to go home

**FAC:** Forward Air Controller (See Bird Dog)

**Gooks:** Slang for an NVA soldier; also could describe any Asian person (considered derogatory)

**Gunship:** A heavily armed helicopter

**Huey:** UH-1 helicopters, flying taxicabs

**I Corps:** Pronounced "eye corps," the northernmost military region of South Vietnam

**KIA:** Killed in action

**KILO:** Captain Kazanowski's call sign; also the letter K in the phonetic alphabet

**LLDB:** Vietnamese Special Forces

**LP:** Listening post

**LRRP:** Long-range reconnaissance patrol; also the freeze-dried meals they carried

**M-16:** Standard assault rifle of American troops

**M-60:** Standard American light machine gun

**M-79:** American single-shot 40 mm grenade launcher

**MACV:** Military Assistance Command Vietnam; advisors to ARVN units

**Medevac:**     Medical evacuation by helicopter

**MIA:**     Missing in action

**Montagnards:**     Ethnic tribal groups living in the highland areas of Vietnam. They were our "paid army"

**MOH:**     Medal of Honor

**MP:**     Military Police

**MPC:**     Military payment certificates used in-country instead of American money

**Nam:**     Vietnam

**NCO:**     Noncommissioned officer

**NVA:**     North Vietnamese Army; also a North Vietnamese soldier

**PT:**     Physical Training

**PX:**     Post Exchange; you could buy almost anything there at a reduced cost

**Point:**     First man on a patrol

**REMF:**     "Rear-Echelon Motherfucker"

**R and R:**     Rest and recuperation, or rest and recreation

**RVN:**     Republic of Vietnam

**S-1:**          Personnel and admin

**S-2:**          Intelligence

**S-3:**          Operations

**Sappers:**      Enemy demolition/assault teams

**SF:**           Special Forces

**SKS:**          An NVA semiautomatic carbine. We could take it home

**SOG:**          Studies and Observation Group. The name used by our cross-border operations

**TAC Air:**      Close air support provided by mainly air force, but occasionally navy

**TAC Officers:** Newly graduated lieutenants who were assigned to help train OCS cadets

**TOC:**          Tactical Operations Center

**VC:**           Vietcong

**WIA:**          Wounded in Action

**XO:**           Executive Officer

Made in the USA
Las Vegas, NV
12 May 2022